Taste*of*Home
Chocolate

THIS BOOK IS GIVEN TO

T0033848

WITH SWEET THOUGHTS FROM:

TASTE OF HOME BOOKS • RDA ENTHUSIAST BRANDS, LLC • MILWAUKEE, WI

Visit us at **tasteofhome.com** for other Taste of Home books and products.

ISBN: 978-1-62145-527-1
LOCC: 2020942850

Executive Editor: Mark Hagen
Senior Art Director: Raeann Thompson
Designer: Jazmin Delgado
Deputy Editor, Copy Desk:
Dulcie Shoener

Cover Photography:
Photographer: Dan Roberts
Set Stylist: Stacey Genaw
Food Stylist: Josh Rink

Pictured on front cover:
Three-Layer Chocolate
Ganache Cake, p. 103

Pictured on spine: Double
Chocolate Fondue, p. 18

Pictured on back cover:
Double Chocolate Martini, p. 9;
Irish Creme Chocolate Trifle, p. 161;
Chocolate & Raspberry Cheesecake,
p. 174; Chocolate Pecan Skillet Cookie,
p. 205; Dark Chocolate Pumpkin
Truffles, p. 27

Printed in China
1 3 5 7 9 10 8 6 4 2

TABLE OF CONTENTS

More ways to connect with us:
SHOPTASTEOFHOME.COM

Indulge in More Than 100 Chocolate Sensations

If there's one ingredient that could be called a gift from heaven, it's chocolate. So when it came time to put together a mini book of our sweetest sensations, the experts in the *Taste of Home* Test Kitchen jumped at the chance. After all, not only is chocolate the star of incredible cakes, brownies, cookies and candies, but it adds sublime flavor to snacks, cocktails and so many other irresistible favorites.

After taste-testing, munching, crunching, sipping and sampling, we created this collection of 116 blissful delights.

We're thrilled to share these divine specialties with you in this all-new cookbook...**Chocolate.**

It's loaded with plenty of recipes for fudge, bark, truffles and the other indulgences you'd expect from a chocolate cookbook, and you'll also find frosty favorites, sweet appetizers, cost-saving gifts, quick breads and oh-so-creamy cheesecakes.

From impressive cakes and pies to dozens of bakeshop staples, the perfect treat is here—starring everyone's favorite ingredient, chocolate!

CHOCOLATE THROUGH THE AGES

From the turn of the century to today, the popularity of this sweet specialty has never waned.

SMART COOKIE
Ruth Graves Wakefield bakes the first chocolate chip cookie at her Toll House Inn in Whitman, Massachusetts. As the story goes, she ran out of baker's chocolate and added broken bits of sweet chocolate to her cookies, assuming they would melt. We're glad they didn't.

ALL IN!
Cocoa production costs drop; chocolate is no longer a pleasure reserved for the rich.

LIFE BEGINS HERE
The first chocolate brownie debuts in a cookbook to raise money for a YMCA in Bangor, Maine. (Try our favorite brownies starting on page 52.)

1895	1900	1907	1914	1930	1930s

HELLO, HERSHEY
Milton Hershey begins developing his milk chocolate bar in Hershey, Pennsylvania.

KISS ME NOW
The very first Hershey's Kiss comes off the assembly line. Today, there are many flavors.

NEW KID ON THE BLOCK
Nestle begins making white chocolate (originally under the name Galak), primarily from cocoa butter, sugar and milk. Whether or not it's true chocolate remains debatable today.

Perfect Pairings 🤎

Wine and chocolate are an ideal match. Here are some of our favorite combos.

MOSCATO D'ASTI
Light and sweet, with a hint of bubbles and a slight orange flavor

Pairs well with
White chocolate; orange-flavored chocolate; orange candy or kumquats dipped in semisweet chocolate

CRANBERRY WINE
Both sweet and tart, with intense cranberry flavor

Pairs well with
Rich, buttery dark chocolate truffles (the darker the better)

ASTI SPUMANTE
Sweet and sparkling, with aromas of flowers and ripe summer fruits

Pairs well with
Dried apricots or pretzels dipped in bittersweet chocolate; sea foam candy

TAWNY PORT
Caramelly and nutty with hints of cinnamon and clove

Pairs well with
Chocolate hazelnut truffles, chocolate cashew clusters, chocolate cheese

BRACHETTO D'ACQUI
This chocolate pairing all-star is slightly sweet and effervescent, with strawberry and red fruit flavors

Pairs well with
Sampler of assorted chocolates; strawberries dipped in chocolate

PARTY TIME!
Guests will swoon over delish options for drizzling on ice cream, coffee or waffles. Fill a slow cooker one-third full with hot water. Set temp to high; leave the lid off. Add wide-mouthed Mason jars filled with chocolate pieces, being careful to keep water from getting in the jars. Chocolate will be melted in about 30 minutes.

BUTTONED UP
U.S. soldiers carry little tubes of candy-coated chocolate buttons with them as they head off to battle in World War II. For the duration of the war, these "M&M's" were available only to the military.

MORE, PLEASE
A study is published noting the cardiovascular benefits of some cocoas and chocolate products.

CHOCOHOLICS
Americans consume 20% of the world's cocoa, with the average American eating about 12 pounds of chocolate per year.

1941 — **1946** — **2006** — **2010** — **TODAY**

A WORTHY ADDITION
Chocolate is in short supply during World War II because of rationing. To keep his business going, Italian chocolatier Pietro Ferrero uses hazelnut as a filler in his formula, thus introducing Nutella to the world.

THE ART OF CHOCOLATE
Artisanal chocolate becomes a thing, with brands such as Vosges Haute Chocolates (Chicago), Mast Brothers Chocolates (Brooklyn, New York) and Theo Chocolate (Seattle) creating unique confections starring surprising ingredients, like wasabi, jalapenos and bacon. (Try our Chocolate-Covered Bacon skewers as seen on pages 200-201.)

TO NIBBLE OR BAKE?

Selecting the right type of chocolate is key to experiencing everything this dreamy indulgence has to offer. Here's what you need to know.

BITTERSWEET
CHOCOLATE

NATURAL
UNSWEETENED
COCOA POWDER

SEMISWEET
CHOCOLATE

DUTCH-PROCESSED
COCOA POWDER

UNSWEETENED CHOCOLATE

UNSWEETENED CHOCOLATE

Chocolate in its simplest form, this variety is also known as baking or bitter chocolate. Unsweetened chocolate has no sugars or added flavors, hence the "bitter" label. And while it's not intended for eating out of hand, it serves as a key ingredient in brownies, cakes and cookies.

NATURAL UNSWEETENED COCOA POWDER

Press most of the cocoa butter out of unsweetened chocolate, and you'll end up with natural unsweetened cocoa powder. This is your secret weapon for deep, rich chocolate flavor in baked goods such as devil's food. While a little may be used on its own to decorate a truffle, cocoa powder is intended for use in recipes, not by the spoonful. Try it plain and you'll quickly understand why.

DUTCH-PROCESSED COCOA POWDER

Also known as alkalized cocoa powder, this type of chocolate has been treated to reduce its acidity, giving it a smoother flavor and a reddish hue. For candy and sauce recipes that call for cocoa powder, you can use Dutch-processed and natural cocoa interchangeably. When it comes to baked goods, though, you'll want to stick to what the recipe calls for, as it can impact the way the sweet treat rises.

BITTERSWEET CHOCOLATE

This is where things can get a little confusing. While the FDA mandates that bittersweet and semisweet chocolate contain at least 35% pure chocolate (cocoa), it doesn't say exactly what those percentages must be. In general, the higher the percentage, the less sweet it will be. Chocolate labeled 60% or 72% cocoa is often referred to as bittersweet. At any percentage, this type is tasty straight up (in candies and bars) or in baked goods.

SEMISWEET CHOCOLATE

Semisweet chocolates (think chocolate chips) generally consist of between 35% and 55% cocoa. The flavor tends to be sweeter and less intense than bittersweet chocolate, which makes this variety ideal for treats such as chocolate chip cookies, where chocolate isn't intended to be the dominant flavor.

MILK CHOCOLATE

Mild in flavor and the sweetest of the true chocolates, milk chocolate contains at least 10% cocoa and usually contains lots of cocoa butter and sugar. Common in candy, it's also a great ingredient to use in recipes where chocolate has a supporting role.

WHITE CHOCOLATE

In the chocolate world, white chocolate has probably caused the most controversy. True chocolate, according to the FDA, must contain at least some chocolate solids—but these are removed to make white chocolate. White chocolate fans argue that since cocoa butter comes from the cocoa bean, white chocolate is true chocolate, too. No matter which side you're on, this variety is enjoyable both in candy and dessert forms.

MILK CHOCOLATE

WHITE CHOCOLATE

Double Chocolate Martini

Is it a beverage or a dessert? Don't let its looks fool you:
This chocolate martini is potent but good!
—*Deborah Williams, Peoria, AZ*

TAKES: 5 MIN. • **MAKES:** 1 SERVING

Grated chocolate
1 maraschino cherry
Chocolate syrup,
  optional
Ice cubes
2½ oz. half-and-half cream
1½ oz. vodka
1½ oz. chocolate liqueur
1½ oz. creme de cacao

1. Sprinkle grated chocolate onto a plate. Moisten the rim of a martini glass with water; hold glass upside down and dip rim into chocolate. Place cherry in glass. If desired, garnish glass with chocolate syrup.

2. Fill a mixing glass or tumbler three-fourths full with ice. Add the cream, vodka, chocolate liqueur and creme de cacao; stir until condensation forms on outside of glass. Strain into glass; serve immediately.

1 MARTINI: 717 cal., 8g fat (5g sat. fat), 38mg chol., 49mg sod., 60g carb. (26g sugars, 0 fiber), 3g pro.

SWEET SECRET
You can also coat the edge of the glass rim with cocoa powder, sugar or chocolate syrup.

Chocolate-Covered Cheese with Black Sea Salt

Every time I make these for guests, people rave about them. They're surprising as an addition to an appetizer table or even served after dinner paired with a nice cabernet or port.
—*Dorothy McNett, Pacific Grove, CA*

PREP: 45 MIN. + STANDING • **MAKES:** 6½ DOZEN

8 oz. aged cheddar or Monterey Jack cheese
6 oz. bittersweet chocolate, chopped
Black sea salt

Cut cheese into ½-in. cubes. In a microwave, melt chocolate; stir until smooth. Dip the cheese cubes in chocolate, allowing excess to drip off. Place on waxed paper. Sprinkle each with a few grains of salt. Let stand until set.

1 PIECE: 24 cal., 2g fat (1g sat. fat), 3mg chol., 19mg sod., 0 carb. (0 sugars, 0 fiber), 1g pro.

READER REVIEW
"Great alternate to sweets! Love the combination of cheddar and dark chocolate. The sprinkle of coarse kosher salt was perfect."
—DIANA, TASTEOFHOME.COM

Mocha Mint Coffee

This doctored-up coffee benefits from hints of mint, cocoa and cinnamon.
And the mini marshmallows bring out the youngster in anyone!
—*Mindie Hilton, Susanville, CA*

PREP: 10 MIN. • COOK: 2 HOURS • MAKES: 8 SERVINGS

6 **cups hot brewed coffee**
2 **packets instant
hot cocoa mix**
½ **cup dulce de leche**
¼ **cup peppermint crunch
baking chips or mint
chocolate chips**
4 **tsp. sugar**
1 **cup miniature
marshmallows**
½ **tsp. ground cinnamon**

1. In a 3-qt. slow cooker, combine first 5 ingredients. Cook, covered, on low until hot, 2-3 hours.

2. Ladle into mugs. Top with mini marshmallows; sprinkle with cinnamon.

¾ CUP: 155 cal., 5g fat (3g sat. fat), 5mg chol., 105mg sod., 27g carb. (24g sugars, 0 fiber), 2g pro.

Chocolate Chip Dip

Is there a kid alive (or a kid at heart) who wouldn't gobble up this creamy dip for
graham crackers? It beats dunking them in milk, hands down!
—*Heather Koenig, Prairie du Chien, WI*

TAKES: 15 MIN. • MAKES: 2 CUPS

1 **pkg. (8 oz.) cream
cheese, softened**
½ **cup butter, softened**
¾ **cup confectioners'
sugar**
2 **Tbsp. brown sugar**
1 **tsp. vanilla extract**
1 **cup miniature
semisweet
chocolate chips
Graham cracker sticks**

In a small bowl, beat cream cheese and butter until light and fluffy. Add the sugars and vanilla; beat until smooth. Stir in chocolate chips. Serve with graham cracker sticks.

2 TBSP.: 180 cal., 14g fat (9g sat. fat), 31mg chol., 84mg sod., 14g carb. (13g sugars, 1g fiber), 2g pro.

SWEET SECRET
For a butter pecan/butter brickle dip, stir in toasted pecans and toffee bits.

Rich Hot Chocolate

Each February my friends and I gather for an outdoor show called Mittenfest. We skip the Bloody Marys and fill our thermoses with this hot cocoa instead. Try the variations, too.
—*Gina Nistico, Denver, CO*

TAKES: 15 MIN. • MAKES: 2 SERVINGS

2/3 **cup heavy whipping cream**
1 **cup 2% milk**
4 **oz. dark chocolate candy bar, chopped**
3 **Tbsp. sugar**
Vanilla rum, optional
Sweetened heavy whipping cream, whipped

NOTES

In a small saucepan, heat heavy whipping cream, milk, chocolate and sugar over medium heat just until mixture comes to a simmer, stirring constantly. Remove from heat; stir until smooth. If desired, add rum. Pour into 2 mugs; top with sweetened whipped cream.

1 CUP: 653 cal., 49g fat (32g sat. fat), 107mg chol., 79mg sod., 60g carb. (56g sugars, 4g fiber), 9g pro.

PUMPKIN-SPICED COCOA: Heat 2/3 cup heavy cream, 1 cup milk, 1/2 cup white baking chips, 2 Tbsp. canned pumpkin and 1 tsp. pumpkin pie spice over medium heat just until mixture comes to a simmer, stirring constantly. Remove from the heat; stir until smooth. If desired, add 3 oz. Rumchata liqueur.

TOASTED COCONUT COCOA: Heat 1 can coconut milk, 1/2 cup milk, 2/3 cup chocolate chips and 2 Tbsp. sugar over medium heat just until mixture comes to a simmer, stirring constantly. Remove from heat; stir until smooth. If desired, add 3 oz. Malibu rum.

SPICY CINNAMON COCOA: Heat 2/3 cup heavy cream, 1 cup milk, 2/3 cup chocolate chips, 2 Tbsp. sugar, 1 tsp. ground cinnamon and 1/8 tsp. cayenne pepper over medium heat just until mixture comes to a simmer, stirring constantly. Remove from heat; stir until smooth. If desired, add 3 oz. cinnamon whiskey.

CHOCOLATE-ORANGE COCOA: Heat 2/3 cup heavy cream, 1 cup milk, 2/3 cup chocolate chips, 2 Tbsp. sugar and 1 tsp. grated orange zest over medium heat just until mixture comes to a simmer, stirring constantly. Remove from heat; stir until smooth. If desired, add 3 oz. Cointreau liqueur.

Chocolate Espresso Martini

For extra flair, drizzle chocolate syrup on the inside of the glass.
—Taste of Home *Test Kitchen*

TAKES: 5 MIN. • **MAKES:** 1 SERVING

Ice cubes
2½ oz. chocolate liqueur
½ oz. brewed espresso
½ oz. vanilla-flavored
vodka
Coarse sugar
1 tsp. chocolate syrup

1. Fill a mixing glass or tumbler three-fourths full with ice. Add the chocolate liqueur, espresso and vodka; stir until condensation forms on outside of glass.

2. Sprinkle sugar on a plate. Moisten the rim of a chilled cocktail glass with water; hold glass upside down and dip rim into sugar. Drizzle chocolate syrup on the inside of glass. Strain vodka mixture into glass.

1 SERVING: 342 cal., 0 fat, 0 chol.,12mg sod., 45g carb. (37g sugars, 0 fiber), 0 pro.

Turtle Chips

Salty-sweet, crunchy-chewy—so many sensations in one delectable bite. This is the absolute easiest recipe to make! Both kids and adults will be reaching for this goodie.
—*Leigh Ann Stewart, Hopkinsville, KY*

TAKES: 25 MIN. • **MAKES:** 16 SERVINGS

1 pkg. (11 oz.) ridged
potato chips
1 pkg. (14 oz.) caramels
⅓ cup heavy whipping
cream
1 pkg. (11½ oz.) milk
chocolate chips
2 Tbsp. shortening
1 cup finely chopped
pecans

1. Arrange whole potato chips in a single layer on a large platter. In a large saucepan, combine caramels and cream. Cook and stir over medium-low heat until caramels are melted. Drizzle over chips.

2. In a microwave, melt chocolate and shortening; stir until smooth. Drizzle over the caramel mixture; sprinkle with pecans. Serve immediately.

½ CUP: 396 cal., 24g fat (7g sat. fat), 13mg chol., 223mg sod., 43g carb. (27g sugars, 2g fiber), 5g pro.

Chocolate Mocha Dusted Almonds

I love to make recipes with nuts. These are chocolaty with a hint of coffee—elegant and addictive! I give them away as gifts; I've even made them for wedding favors.
—*Annette Scholz, Medaryville, IN*

PREP: 20 MIN. + CHILLING • MAKES: 12 SERVINGS

1 cup dark chocolate
   chips
2 cups toasted whole
   almonds
¾ cup confectioners'
   sugar
3 Tbsp. baking cocoa
4½ tsp. instant coffee
   granules

1. Microwave chocolate chips, covered, at 50% power, stirring once or twice, until melted, 3-4 minutes. Stir until smooth. Add almonds; mix until coated.

2. Meanwhile, combine remaining ingredients. Transfer almonds to sugar mixture; toss to coat evenly. Spread over a waxed paper-lined baking sheet.

3. Refrigerate until chocolate is set. Store in an airtight container in refrigerator.

ABOUT 3 TBSP.: 270 cal., 19g fat (5g sat. fat), 0 chol., 12mg sod., 25g carb. (19g sugars, 4g fiber), 7g pro.

SWEET SECRETS
- Like spice? Add ½ tsp. ground chipotle pepper or chili powder.
- Try this with any kind of nut. Just make sure you toast them first to bring out all their flavor.

Double Chocolate Fondue

Thick, rich and luscious, this yummy dip won't last long. I eat spoonfuls right out of the refrigerator! Try it with pretzel sticks or graham crackers for dippers.
—*Cindy Stetzer, Alliance, OH*

TAKES: 20 MIN. • **MAKES:** 2¼ CUPS

1   cup sugar
2   cans (5 oz. each) evaporated milk, divided
½   cup baking cocoa
4   oz. unsweetened chocolate, chopped
2   Tbsp. butter
1   tsp. vanilla extract
      Cubed pound cake and assorted fresh fruit

1. In a small saucepan, combine sugar and 1 can milk. Cook over low heat, stirring occasionally, until sugar is dissolved.

2. In a small bowl, whisk cocoa and the remaining milk until smooth. Add to the sugar mixture; bring to a boil, whisking constantly.

3. Remove from the heat; stir in chocolate and butter until melted. Stir in the vanilla. Keep warm. Serve with cubed cake and fruit.

¼ CUP: 244 cal., 12g fat (7g sat. fat), 17mg chol., 53mg sod., 32g carb. (26g sugars, 3g fiber), 5g pro.

READER REVIEW
"We loved this; all I had was blocks of semisweet chocolate and it was perfect. My 3-year-old said, 'Mommy, this is the best dessert I ever had!'"
—JOSEYSMOMMY, TASTEOFHOME.COM

How to Make Any Chocolate Fondue

Get creative when you serve up your own creamy treat. Simply follow these easy steps.

- Combine chopped chocolates and cream or evaporated milk in a heavy saucepan. Cook, stirring constantly, over low heat until smooth.

- Stir in juice concentrate, wine or a bit of extract to taste. Keep the mixture warm.

- Serve with berries, melon, crackers, cake cubes, cookies or other dippers.

Cranberry Dark Chocolate Trail Mix

A close friend once gave me a jar of trail mix that was absolutely delicious. My re-creation comes pretty close to the original and is truly one of my favorite snacks!
—*Nancy Johnson, Laverne, OK*

TAKES: 5 MIN. • **MAKES:** 6 CUPS

1 pkg. (10 oz.) dark chocolate chips
1½ cups dried cranberries (about 8 oz.)
1½ cups sliced almonds
1 cup raisins
1 cup coarsely chopped walnuts
½ cup pistachios

Toss together all ingredients. Store in airtight containers.

¼ CUP: 176 cal., 11g fat (3g sat. fat), 0 chol., 16mg sod., 21g carb. (15g sugars, 3g fiber), 3g pro.

Chocolate Martini

The variations on martinis seem endless. But this sweet version is both creative and sophisticated in taste and presentation. It's a classy way to finish or even start a meal.
—Taste of Home *Test Kitchen*

TAKES: 5 MIN. • **MAKES:** 1 SERVING

Ice cubes
2 oz. vodka
2 oz. creme de cacao or chocolate liqueur

GARNISH
Chocolate shavings, white chocolate curl or chocolate truffle

Fill a mixing glass or tumbler three-fourths full with ice. Add vodka and creme de cacao; stir until condensation forms on outside of glass. Strain into a chilled cocktail glass. Garnish as desired.

⅔ CUP: 378 cal., 0 fat (0 sat. fat), 0 chol., 5mg sod., 28g carb. (28g sugars, 0 fiber), 0 pro.

CREAMY CHOCOLATE MARTINI: Stir 1-2 oz. half-and-half cream with the vodka and creme de cacao. Strain into a chocolate syrup-drizzled cocktail glass if desired.

Chocolate Fruit Dip

I usually serve this popular dip with strawberries and pineapple, but it's good with other fruit, such as apples and melon. Your friends will think this one's really special.
—*Sarah Maury Swan, Granite, MD*

TAKES: 10 MIN. • MAKES: 2 CUPS

1 pkg. (8 oz.) cream cheese, softened
⅓ cup sugar
⅓ cup baking cocoa
1 tsp. vanilla extract
2 cups whipped topping
Assorted fruit for dipping

In a large bowl, beat the cream cheese and sugar until smooth. Beat in cocoa and vanilla. Beat in whipped topping until smooth. Serve with fruit.

2 TBSP.: 96 cal., 7g fat (5g sat. fat), 16mg chol., 42mg sod., 8g carb. (5g sugars, 0 fiber), 1g pro.

S'mores No-Bake Bites

There's no easier way to get that s'mores goodness in your kitchen. Mix these cookies together and chill till you're ready to share.
—*Taste of Home Test Kitchen*

PREP: 15 MIN. + CHILLING • MAKES: 2½ DOZEN

1⅔ cups milk chocolate chips
2 Tbsp. canola oil
3 cups Golden Grahams
2 cups miniature marshmallows

In a large microwave-safe bowl, microwave chocolate chips and oil, uncovered, at 50% power until chocolate is melted, stirring every 30 seconds, 1-1½ minutes. Stir in cereal until blended; fold in marshmallows. Drop by rounded tablespoonfuls onto waxed paper-lined baking sheets. Refrigerate until firm, about 15 minutes.

1 BITE: 79 cal., 4g fat (2g sat. fat), 2mg chol., 39mg sod., 11g carb. (8g sugars, 1g fiber), 1g pro.

Striped Chocolate Popcorn

Inspired by chocolate popcorn at a candy shop, I decided to try something a little different for a bake sale. Sweet, salty and crunchy, it proved to be a recipe for success.

—Mary Schmittinger, Colgate, WI

PREP: 15 MIN. + STANDING • **MAKES:** 17 CUPS

12 **cups popped popcorn**
2 **cups miniature pretzels**
1 **cup pecan halves, toasted**
¼ **cup butter, melted**
4 **oz. white candy coating, coarsely chopped**
2 **oz. milk chocolate candy coating, coarsely chopped**

1. In a large bowl, combine the popcorn, pretzels and pecans. Drizzle with butter and toss; set aside.

2. In a microwave, melt white candy coating at 70% power for 1 minute; stir. Microwave at additional 10- to 20-second intervals, stirring until smooth. Drizzle over popcorn mixture; toss to coat. Spread on foil-lined baking sheets.

3. In a microwave, melt milk chocolate coating; stir until smooth. Drizzle over popcorn mixture. Let stand in a cool place until chocolate is set. Store in an airtight container.

1 CUP: 177 cal., 12g fat (5g sat. fat), 7mg chol., 170mg sod., 16g carb. (7g sugars, 2g fiber), 2g pro.

NOTES

_____
_____
_____
_____
_____
_____
_____
_____
_____
_____

CHAPTER 2
Fudge, Truffles & More

Dark Chocolate Pumpkin Truffles

What an inviting combo of flavors—and the fact that these bites
come together easily makes them even more special.
—*Monica Mooney, Roseville, CA*

PREP: 30 MIN. + FREEZING • MAKES: 2½ DOZEN

⅔ cup reduced-fat
   cream cheese
½ cup confectioners'
   sugar
⅔ cup canned pumpkin
1 tsp. pumpkin pie spice
1 tsp. vanilla extract
2¼ cups crushed reduced-
   fat graham crackers
1 pkg. (10 oz.) dark
   chocolate chips

1. In a small bowl, beat cream cheese and confectioners'
sugar until blended. Beat in pumpkin, pie spice and vanilla.
Stir in cracker crumbs. Freeze, covered, 20 minutes or
until firm enough to shape.

2. Shape pumpkin mixture into 1-in. balls; place on waxed
paper-lined baking sheets. Freeze 20 minutes or until firm.

3. In a microwave, melt chocolate; stir until smooth. Dip
truffles in chocolate; allow excess to drip off. Return
to baking sheets; refrigerate until set. Store in airtight
containers in the refrigerator.

1 TRUFFLE: 97 cal., 5g fat (3g sat. fat), 4mg chol., 60mg sod.,
13g carb. (8g sugars, 1g fiber), 2g pro.

To-Do's (and Ta-Da's)
All you need are a fork
and a knife to keep dipping
mess-free. Drop fillings in
chocolate, scoop out with a
fork and roll off with a knife.

Nana's Rocky Road

We make rocky road-style fudge every Christmas and it's a tradition,
but why wait until the holidays for chocolate this good?
—*Ashley Berry, Montgomery Village, Maryland*

PREP: 15 MIN. • **COOK:** 5 MIN. + CHILLING • **MAKES:** ABOUT 2½ LBS. (48 PIECES)

1½ tsp. plus 1 Tbsp. butter,
   divided
2 cups semisweet
   chocolate chips
1 can (14 oz.) sweetened
   condensed milk
2 cups salted peanuts,
   plus more for topping
1 pkg. (10 oz.) miniature
   marshmallows, plus
   more for topping

1. Line a 13x9-in. baking pan with foil, letting ends extend over sides by 1 in. Grease the foil with 1½ tsp. butter; set aside.

2. In a large saucepan, combine chocolate chips, milk and the remaining butter. Cook and stir over medium heat until mixture is smooth. Remove from the heat; stir in 2 cups peanuts. Place the marshmallows in a large bowl; add chocolate mixture and stir well. Spread into prepared pan. Sprinkle with additional peanuts and marshmallows. Refrigerate until firm.

3. Using foil, lift fudge out of pan. Cut into 1½-in. squares.

1 PIECE: 153 cal., 8g fat (4g sat. fat), 4mg chol., 39mg sod., 20g carb. (16g sugars, 1g fiber), 3g pro.

Chocolate Peanut Butter Candy

With only three ingredients, these chocolate-swirl treats take just moments to whip up!
If you have little ones visiting, have them help you with the stirring.
—*Holly Demers, Abbotsford, BC*

PREP: 10 MIN. + CHILLING • **MAKES:** ABOUT 2½ LBS. (40 SERVINGS)

1 **lb. white candy coating, coarsely chopped**
1½ **cups creamy peanut butter**
2 **cups semisweet chocolate chips**

1. In a large microwave-safe bowl, melt candy coating; stir until smooth. Stir in peanut butter; thinly spread onto a waxed paper-lined baking sheet.

2. In another microwave-safe bowl, melt chocolate chips; stir until smooth. Drizzle over candy coating mixture; cut through mixture with a knife to swirl the chocolate. Chill until firm.

3. Break into pieces. Store in an airtight container in the refrigerator.

1 OZ.: 156 cal., 11g fat (6g sat. fat), 0 chol., 42mg sod., 16g carb. (13g sugars,1g fiber), 3g pro.

READER REVIEW
"Wow! This is so delicious! And it could not be easier to make. I will be making this from now on as my signature homemade gift for co-workers, friends and family. Thanks so much for an awesome, delicious, super easy recipe."
—SUZETTE316, TASTEOFHOME.COM

Mixed Nut Clusters

Serve these with hot chocolate for a real chocolate overload! They also make standout gifts. I box them up, setting each cluster in a foil or paper candy cup.
—*Ida Tuey, South Lyon, MI*

PREP: 30 MIN. + CHILLING • MAKES: 6 DOZEN

2 cups semisweet
   chocolate chips
1 can (14 oz.) sweetened
   condensed milk
1 Tbsp. honey
1 Tbsp. vanilla extract
1 cup each chopped
   walnuts, cashews,
   pecans and almonds

1. In a large heavy saucepan, melt chocolate chips, milk and honey over low heat; stir until blended. Remove from heat. Stir in vanilla; add nuts.

2. Drop by rounded tablespoonfuls onto waxed paper-lined baking sheets. Refrigerate until firm. Store in refrigerator.

1 PIECE: 85 cal., 6g fat (2g sat. fat), 2mg chol., 20mg sod., 8g carb. (6g sugars, 1g fiber), 2g pro. **DIABETIC EXCHANGES:** 1 fat, ½ starch.

No-Bake Chocolate Cookie Triangles

When you want a special treat but time is short, try these no-bake bars. You need only a few minutes to make the rich, chocolaty and oh-so-good bites.
—*Linda Stemen, Monroeville, IN*

PREP: 15 MIN. + CHILLING • MAKES: 32 COOKIES

¾ cup butter, cubed
8 oz. semisweet
   chocolate, chopped
20 vanilla wafers,
   coarsely crushed
½ cup chopped pecans

1. In a microwave, melt butter and chocolate; stir until smooth. Cool slightly. Stir in wafer crumbs and pecans. Transfer to a greased, foil-lined 8-in. square pan. Cover and refrigerate for 2 hours or until firm.

2. Using foil, lift chocolate out of pan. Discard foil; cut into 32 triangles. Refrigerate leftovers.

1 TRIANGLE: 96 cal., 8g fat (4g sat. fat), 12mg chol., 38mg sod., 6g carb. (4g sugars, 1g fiber), 1g pro.

Stuffed Cherries Dipped in Chocolate

I make these delectable cherry treats in early summer when the cherries are ripe and plentiful. A summertime favorite, they freeze very nicely and are a wonderful treat to serve later in the season.
—*Judy Bond, Duncan, BC*

PREP: 45 MIN. • MAKES: 5 DOZEN

1½ lbs. fresh dark sweet cherries with stems
1 pkg. (8 oz.) cream cheese, softened
2 Tbsp. ground hazelnuts
2 Tbsp. maple syrup
2 cups white baking chips
12 tsp. shortening, divided
1½ cups milk chocolate chips
1½ cups semisweet chocolate chips

1. Pit cherries through the sides, leaving stems intact. In a small bowl, beat cream cheese until smooth. Stir in hazelnuts and syrup. Pipe into cherries.

2. In a small microwave-safe bowl, melt white chips and 5 tsp. shortening at 70% power. Microwave at additional 10- to 20-second intervals, stirring until smooth. In another bowl, repeat with milk chocolate chips and 3½ tsp. shortening. Repeat with semisweet chips and remaining shortening.

3. Holding stems, dip a third of the stuffed cherries into melted white chocolate; allow excess to drip off. Place on waxed paper; let stand until set. Repeat with remaining cherries and milk chocolate and semisweet chocolate. Dip the white-coated cherries a second time to completely cover; let stand until set.

4. Reheat remaining melted chocolate if necessary. Drizzle white chocolate over cherries dipped in milk or semisweet chocolate. Drizzle milk or semisweet chocolate over white chocolate-dipped cherries. Store in an airtight container in the refrigerator.

1 CHOCOLATE-DIPPED CHERRY: 105 cal., 7g fat (4g sat. fat), 6mg chol., 20mg sod., 11g carb. (10g sugars, 1g fiber), 1g pro. **DIABETIC EXCHANGES:** 1 starch, 1 fat.

NOTES

_____
_____
_____
_____
_____
_____
_____
_____
_____
_____
_____
_____
_____

Triple Chocolate Fudge

This recipe makes more than enough to share with family and friends.
With three types of chocolate, it's the ultimate fudge.
—*Linette Shepherd, Williamston, MI*

PREP: 20 MIN. • COOK: 25 MIN. + CHILLING • MAKES: 6¾ LBS. (234 PIECES)

4 tsp. plus ½ cup butter, divided
4½ cups sugar
1 can (12 oz.) evaporated milk
1 tsp. salt
16 oz. German sweet chocolate, chopped
2 cups semisweet chocolate chips
1 pkg. (11½ oz.) milk chocolate chips
2 jars (7 oz. each) marshmallow creme
4 cups chopped pecans or walnuts, toasted
2 tsp. vanilla extract

1. Line two 13x9-in. pans with foil and grease the foil with 4 tsp. butter. In a heavy Dutch oven, combine sugar, milk, salt and the remaining butter. Bring to a boil over medium heat, stirring constantly. Cook, without stirring, until a candy thermometer reads 234° (soft-ball stage).

2. Remove from the heat. Stir in the chopped German chocolate and the semisweet and milk chocolate chips until smooth. Fold in the marshmallow creme, pecans and vanilla. Spread into prepared pans.

3. Refrigerate for 1 hour or until firm. Using foil, lift fudge out of pans. Discard foil; cut fudge into 1-in. squares. Store in airtight containers.

1 PIECE: 64 cal., 3g fat (1g sat. fat), 2mg chol., 17mg sod., 9g carb. (8g sugars, 0 fiber), 1g pro. **DIABETIC EXCHANGES:** ½ starch, ½ fat.

SWEET SECRET
Test your candy thermometer before each use by bringing water to a boil; the thermometer should read 212°. Adjust the recipe temperature up or down based on the test.

Oreos & Candy Cane Chocolate Bark

There are so many incredible surprises in this festive bark, including dark chocolate, cream-filled cookies and candy canes.
—*Robin Turner, Lake Elsinore, CA*

PREP: 15 MIN. + CHILLING • **MAKES:** 1½ LBS. (24 SERVINGS)

2 pkg. (10 oz. each) dark chocolate chips
10 candy cane or chocolate mint creme Oreo cookies, split and chopped
⅓ cup white baking chips
⅛ tsp. peppermint extract
2 candy canes, crushed

1. Line a 15x10x1-in. baking pan with parchment. In the top of a double boiler or a metal bowl over hot water, melt dark chocolate; stir until smooth. Remove from heat. Stir in cookies; spread over prepared pan.

2. Microwave white baking chips on high until melted, stirring every 30 seconds. Stir in extract. Drizzle over dark chocolate mixture; sprinkle with crushed candy canes. Cool. Refrigerate until set, about 1 hour.

3. Break into pieces. Store in an airtight container.

1 OZ.: 158 cal., 9g fat (6g sat. fat), 1mg chol., 36mg sod., 21g carb. (18g sugars, 2g fiber), 2g pro.

> **SWEET SECRET**
> If the bark hardens too quickly, you may have trouble getting toppings to stick. Try popping the pan into a warm oven for a minute to soften the chocolate before adding toppings.

Creamy Peppermint Patties

Like a little sweet after a meal but don't want a full dessert? Maybe you're looking for a chocolaty midnight snack? These chocolate candies are always the answer.
—*Donna Gonda, North Canton, OH*

PREP: 40 MIN. + CHILLING • **MAKES:** ABOUT 8 DOZEN

1 pkg. (8 oz.) cream cheese, softened
1 tsp. peppermint extract
9 cups confectioners' sugar
1½ cups milk chocolate chips
1½ cups semisweet chocolate chips
3 Tbsp. shortening

1. Beat cream cheese and extract until smooth. Gradually add confectioners' sugar, beating well.

2. Shape into 1-in. balls. Place on waxed paper-lined baking sheets. Flatten into patties 1½-1¾ in. in diameter. Cover and refrigerate until chilled, about 1 hour.

3. In a microwave, melt chips and shortening; stir until smooth. Cool slightly. Dip patties in melted chocolate, allowing excess to drip off; place on waxed paper until set. Store in the refrigerator.

1 PATTY: 82 cal., 3g fat (2g sat. fat), 3mg chol., 10mg sod., 15g carb. (14g sugars, 0 fiber), 0 pro.

READER REVIEW
"I make these for holidays. They can also be frozen. Very easy to prepare and they are delectable!"
—DOGGIEMOM2, TASTEOFHOME.COM

My Favorite Fudge

My fudge is virtually foolproof and so creamy you won't believe it.
I've searched for years for the richest fudge, and this one does it for me.
You can add just about anything you like to customize it.
—*Barbara Miller, Oakdale, MN*

PREP: 15 MIN. • COOK: 10 MIN. + COOLING • MAKES: 5¾ LBS. (96 PIECES)

4½ cups sugar
1 can (12 oz.) evaporated milk
½ cup butter, cubed
2 pkg. (11½ oz. each) milk chocolate chips
4½ cups miniature marshmallows
2 oz. unsweetened chocolate, chopped
3 cups chopped walnuts, toasted
2 tsp. vanilla extract
4 oz. white baking chocolate, melted

1. Line a 13x9-in. pan with foil; coat with cooking spray.

2. In a heavy Dutch oven, combine sugar, milk and butter. Bring to a rapid boil over medium heat, stirring constantly. Cook and stir 5 minutes. Remove from heat.

3. Stir in chocolate chips, marshmallows and chopped chocolate until melted. Fold in the walnuts and vanilla. Immediately spread into prepared pan. Drizzle with melted white baking chocolate; cool completely.

4. Using foil, lift fudge out of pan. Remove foil; cut fudge into 96 squares. Store between layers of waxed paper in airtight containers.

1 PIECE: 127 cal., 6g fat (2g sat. fat), 6mg chol., 18mg sod., 17g carb. (15g sugars, 1g fiber), 2g pro.

SWEET SECRET
For this recipe, make sure you use evaporated milk, not condensed milk. Sweetened condensed milk is milk with most of the water cooked off, to which sugar has been added. Evaporated milk is concentrated in the same way but doesn't contain added sugar.

Dark Chocolate Bourbon Balls

Here's an all-time chocolate classic made easy.
The blended flavor of bourbon and pecans is always irresistible!
—Taste of Home *Test Kitchen*

PREP: 30 MIN. + CHILLING • **MAKES:** 4 DOZEN

1¼ cups finely chopped
   pecans, **divided**
¼ cup bourbon
½ cup butter, softened
3¾ cups confectioners'
   sugar
1 lb. dark chocolate
   candy coating, melted

1. Combine 1 cup pecans and bourbon; let stand, covered, for 8 hours or overnight.

2. Cream butter and confectioners' sugar, ¼ cup at a time, until crumbly; stir in pecan mixture. Refrigerate, covered, until firm enough to shape into 1-in. balls, about 45 minutes. Place balls on waxed paper-lined baking sheets. Refrigerate until firm, about 1 hour.

3. Dip balls in chocolate coating; allow excess to drip off. Sprinkle with remaining ¼ cup pecans. Let stand until set.

1 BOURBON BALL: 124 cal., 7g fat (4g sat. fat), 5mg chol., 15mg sod., 16g carb. (15g sugars, 0 fiber), 0 pro.

> **SWEET SECRET**
> Dark chocolate not only tastes good, it's good for you, too. It contains iron, fiber, antioxidants and vitamin C. The higher the cacao content (cocoa bean solids, which may be listed as a percentage on the label), the higher the content of these components in the chocolate.

Raspberry-Mocha Chocolate

Give classic chocolate bark a bit of coffee-shop sophistication with crushed espresso beans. Swirls of raspberry and white baking chips make it even more special.
—Aysha Schurman, Ammon, ID

PREP: 10 MIN. + CHILLING • **MAKES:** 1 LB. (16 SERVINGS)

1¼ cups white baking chips
1 tsp. shortening, divided
¼ cup seedless raspberry preserves
4 Tbsp. finely crushed chocolate-covered espresso beans, divided
1 cup plus 2 Tbsp. dark chocolate chips, divided

1. Line a 9-in. square pan with foil; set aside. In a microwave, melt white chips and ½ tsp. shortening; stir until smooth. Spread into prepared pan.

2. Microwave preserves in 10- to 20-second intervals until melted; stir until smooth. Drop preserves by teaspoonfuls over top. Cut through layer with a knife to swirl. Sprinkle with 2 Tbsp. espresso beans. Refrigerate for 10 minutes or until firm.

3. In a microwave, melt 1 cup dark chocolate chips and remaining shortening; stir until smooth. Spread over white chocolate layer. Finely chop remaining dark chocolate chips. Sprinkle chips and remaining espresso beans over the top. Refrigerate until firm. Break into small pieces. Store in an airtight container.

1 OZ.: 173 cal., 10g fat (6g sat. fat), 3mg chol., 18mg sod., 22g carb. (20g sugars, 1g fiber), 2g pro.

Coconut Almond Candy

The secret ingredient in this homemade candy is a true surprise—no one tasting these delicious morsels will guess what's in the sweet, creamy filling!
—Katrina Smith, Lawrence, KS

PREP: 45 MIN. + CHILLING • **MAKES:** 2 DOZEN

2 **cups sweetened shredded coconut**
½ **cup mashed potatoes (with added milk and butter)**
¼ **tsp. vanilla extract**
⅛ **tsp. salt, optional**
2 **cups confectioners' sugar**
24 **unblanched almonds, toasted**
1 **pkg. (11½ oz.) milk chocolate chips**
1 **Tbsp. butter**

1. In a large bowl, mix coconut, potatoes, vanilla and, if desired, salt. Gradually beat in confectioners' sugar. Refrigerate, covered, until firm enough to shape, about 1 hour.

2. With hands dusted with confectioners' sugar, shape mixture into twenty-four 1-in. ovals. Flatten slightly, then wrap each around an almond. Place on waxed paper-lined baking sheets; freeze until firm, at least 30 minutes.

3. In a microwave, melt chocolate chips and butter; stir until smooth. Using a fork, dip candies in chocolate mixture; allow excess to drip off. Return to baking sheets; refrigerate until set. Store between layers of waxed paper in an airtight container in the refrigerator.

1 PIECE: 167 cal., 8g fat (5g sat. fat), 5mg chol., 61mg sod., 23g carb. (20g sugars, 1g fiber), 2g pro.

Mackinac Fudge

When I got married, a woman at my parents' church gave me this version of a popular Michigan treat. I sometimes pipe a bit of frosting onto each piece for cute decoration.
—*Kristen Ekhoff, Akron, IN*

PREP: 5 MIN. • COOK: 25 MIN. + CHILLING • MAKES: 3 LBS. (117 PIECES)

2 tsp. plus 1 cup butter, divided
4 cups sugar
1 cup 2% milk
25 large marshmallows
1 pkg. (11½ oz.) milk chocolate chips
2 cups semisweet chocolate chips
2 oz. unsweetened chocolate, chopped
1 tsp. vanilla extract
Decorating icing and sprinkles, optional

1. Line a 13x9-in. pan with foil; grease the foil with 2 tsp. butter.

2. In a large heavy saucepan, combine the sugar, milk and remaining butter. Bring to a rapid boil over medium heat, stirring constantly. Cook, without stirring, for 2 minutes. Remove from the heat.

3. Stir in marshmallows until melted. Add all chocolate; stir until melted. Stir in vanilla. Immediately spread into prepared pan; cool for 1 hour.

4. Score into 1-in. squares. Refrigerate, covered, for at least 3 hours or until firm. Using foil, lift out fudge. Remove foil; cut fudge. Store between layers of waxed paper in airtight containers. Decorate as desired.

1 PIECE: 79 cal., 4g fat (2g sat. fat), 5mg chol., 18mg sod., 12g carb. (11g sugars, 0 fiber), 1g pro.

NOTES

_____
_____
_____
_____
_____
_____
_____
_____
_____
_____
_____
_____
_____
_____
_____
_____

Coconut-Almond Cookie Bark

As kids, my friends and I sandwiched Almond Joys between cookies.
For our high school reunion, I re-created that idea with a cookie-chocolate bark.
—*Faith Cromwell, San Francisco, CA*

PREP: 25 MIN. + COOLING • **BAKE:** 25 MIN. + COOLING • **MAKES:** ABOUT 2 LBS. (32 SERVINGS)

1   cup butter, cubed
½   cup sugar
½   cup packed
    brown sugar
1   large egg
¾   tsp. almond extract
2   cups all-purpose flour
¾   tsp. salt
1¼ cups sweetened
    shredded coconut,
    divided
1½ cups milk chocolate
    chips, divided
⅓   cup sliced almonds,
    toasted

1. Preheat oven to 375°. In a small heavy saucepan, melt butter over medium heat. Heat 6-8 minutes or until golden brown, stirring constantly. Transfer to a large bowl; cool 15 minutes.

2. Whisk in sugars, egg and extract until smooth. In another bowl, whisk flour and salt; stir into sugar mixture. Fold in 1 cup coconut and ¾ cup chocolate chips. Press into an ungreased 15x10x1-in. baking pan. Bake until golden brown, 24-28 minutes.

3. Transfer pan to a wire rack; sprinkle with remaining chocolate chips. Toast remaining coconut. Spread chocolate chips evenly over cookie. Sprinkle with remaining coconut; top with almonds. Cool completely in pan on a wire rack.

4. Refrigerate 15 minutes or until chocolate is set. Break cookie into pieces.

1 OZ.: 150 cal., 9g fat (5g sat. fat), 20mg chol., 104mg sod., 17g carb. (11g sugars, 1g fiber), 2g pro.

Chocolate Billionaires

Everyone raves about these chocolate and caramel candies. I received the recipe from a friend while living in Texas. When we moved, I made sure this recipe made the trip with me!
—*June Humphrey, Strongsville, OH*

PREP: 45 MIN. + CHILLING • **MAKES:** ABOUT 2 LBS. (32 SERVINGS)

1 pkg. (14 oz.) caramels
3 Tbsp. water
1½ cups chopped pecans
1 cup Rice Krispies
3 cups milk chocolate
   chips
1½ tsp. shortening

SWEET SECRET
Pecans have a higher fat content than other nuts, so they're more prone to going rancid. They'll stay fresh for twice as long in the freezer as they would at room temperature.

1. Line 2 baking sheets with waxed paper; grease the paper and set aside. In a large heavy saucepan, combine the caramels and water; cook and stir over low heat until smooth. Stir in pecans and cereal until coated. Drop by teaspoonfuls onto prepared pans. Refrigerate at least 10 minutes or until firm.

2. Meanwhile, in a microwave, melt chocolate chips and shortening; stir until smooth. Dip candy into chocolate, coating all sides; allow excess to drip off. Place on prepared pans. Refrigerate until set. Store candy in an airtight container.

1 OZ.: 172 cal., 10g fat (4g sat. fat), 4mg chol., 51mg sod., 20g carb. (17g sugars, 1g fiber), 2g pro.

CHAPTER 3
Brownies,
Bars & Cookies

Hot Chocolate Cookies

Using hot chocolate mix and marshmallow bits in the cookie dough
really makes these cookies taste like hot cocoa. Yum!
—*Lisa Kaminski, Wauwatosa, WI*

PREP: 15 MIN. • **BAKE:** 10 MIN./BATCH • **MAKES:** 5 DOZEN

¾ cup butter, softened
¾ cup sugar
¾ cup packed brown
    sugar
2 large eggs, room
    temperature
1 tsp. vanilla extract
2¼ cups all-purpose flour
½ cup instant hot cocoa
    mix (about 3 packets)
3 Tbsp. baking cocoa
1 tsp. salt
1 tsp. baking soda
½ tsp. baking powder
1 cup vanilla
    marshmallow bits
    (not miniature
    marshmallows)
1 cup semisweet
    chocolate chips

1. Preheat oven to 375°. In a large bowl, cream butter and sugars until light and fluffy, 5-7 minutes. Beat in eggs and vanilla. In another bowl, whisk flour, cocoa mix, baking cocoa, salt, baking soda and baking powder; gradually beat into creamed mixture. Gently stir in the marshmallow bits and chocolate chips.

2. Drop dough by tablespoonfuls 2 in. apart onto greased baking sheets. Bake until set, 10-12 minutes. Remove to wire racks to cool completely.

1 COOKIE: 81 cal., 4g fat (2g sat. fat), 12mg chol., 95mg sod., 12g carb. (8g sugars, 0 fiber), 1g pro.

SWEET SECRET
Smaller than miniature marshmallows, marshmallow bits are usually sold in plastic shaker containers. Look for them in the grocery store's baking aisle or near the other marshmallow products.

Chocolate Cheesecake Bars

When you don't have time to bake a chocolate cheesecake, reach for this easy recipe. An almond-flavored dough serves as both crust and topping for a soft fudgy filling.
—*Louise Good, Flemington, NJ*

PREP: 15 MIN. • **BAKE:** 35 MIN. + COOLING • **MAKES:** 4 DOZEN

1   cup butter, softened
1½ cups sugar
2   large eggs, room temperature
½   tsp. almond extract
3   cups all-purpose flour
1   tsp. baking powder
½   tsp. salt

FILLING
2   cups semisweet chocolate chips
1   pkg. (8 oz.) cream cheese
1   can (5 oz.) evaporated milk
1   cup chopped walnuts
½   tsp. almond extract

1. In a large bowl, cream butter and sugar until light and fluffy, 5-7 minutes. Add eggs, 1 at a time, beating well after each addition. Beat in extract. Combine the flour, baking powder and salt; gradually add to the creamed mixture and mix well. Press half the dough onto the bottom of a greased 13x9-in. baking pan. Set aside the remaining dough for the topping.

2. For filling, in a large saucepan, combine the chocolate chips, cream cheese and milk; cook and stir over low heat until smooth. Remove from the heat; stir in walnuts and extract. Spread over dough.

3. Break off small pieces of remaining dough; drop over the filling. Bake at 375° until topping is golden brown, 35-40 minutes. Cool completely on a wire rack. Cut into bars. Refrigerate leftovers.

1 BAR: 160 cal., 9g fat (5g sat. fat), 25mg chol., 92mg sod., 17g carb. (11g sugars, 1g fiber), 3g pro.

READER REVIEW
"These were easy to make, and the almond flavor of the extract really came through."
—MEWOLCOTT412, TASTEOFHOME.COM

Coconut Chocolate Slices

These crispy cookies with a chewy coconut center travel really well. I often sent boxes to my Army son, and he told me they always arrived in perfect condition.
—*Cheri Booth, Gering, NE*

PREP: 30 MIN. + CHILLING • BAKE: 10 MIN. • MAKES: ABOUT 4 DOZEN

3 oz. cream cheese, softened
⅓ cup sugar
1 tsp. vanilla extract
1 cup sweetened shredded coconut
½ cup finely chopped nuts

COOKIE DOUGH
6 Tbsp. butter, softened
1 cup confectioners' sugar
1 large egg, room temperature
2 oz. semisweet chocolate, melted and cooled
1 tsp. vanilla extract
1½ cups all-purpose flour
½ tsp. baking soda
½ tsp. salt

SWEET SECRET
Chopped almonds offer a nice flavor boost to these cookies, but feel free to use whatever nuts you like.

1. Beat cream cheese, granulated sugar and vanilla until smooth. Stir in coconut and nuts. Refrigerate until easy to handle.

2. Meanwhile, cream butter and confectioners' sugar until light and fluffy, 5-7 minutes. Beat in egg, chocolate and vanilla. Combine flour, baking soda and salt; gradually add to creamed mixture and mix well. Refrigerate until easy to handle, about 30 minutes.

3. Roll the dough between waxed paper into a 14x4½-in. rectangle. Remove top piece of waxed paper. Shape the coconut filling into a 14-in. roll; place on dough, 1 in. from a long side. Roll dough around filling and seal edges. Wrap and refrigerate 2-3 hours or overnight.

4. Preheat oven to 350°. Unwrap the dough and cut into ¼-in. slices. Place 2 in. apart on greased baking sheets, reshaping if necessary. Bake until set, 8-10 minutes. Cool 1 minute before removing to wire racks.

1 COOKIE: 75 cal., 4g fat (2g sat. fat), 9mg chol., 61mg sod., 8g carb. (5g sugars, 0 fiber), 1g pro.

Chocolate Fudge Brownies

My children always looked forward to these after-school snacks.
The moist treats are so fudgy they don't need icing.
—*Hazel Fritchie, Palestine, IL*

PREP: 15 MIN. • **BAKE:** 35 MIN. + COOLING • **MAKES:** 16 SERVINGS

1 **cup butter, cubed**
6 **oz. unsweetened chocolate, chopped**
4 **large eggs, room temperature**
2 **cups sugar**
1 **tsp. vanilla extract**
½ **tsp. salt**
1 **cup all-purpose flour**
2 **cups chopped walnuts**
 Confectioners' sugar, optional

1. Preheat oven to 350°. In a small saucepan, melt butter and chocolate over low heat. Cool slightly.

2. In a large bowl, beat eggs, sugar, vanilla and salt until blended. Stir in chocolate mixture. Add flour, mixing well. Stir in walnuts.

3. Spread into a greased 9-in. square baking pan. Bake 35-40 minutes or until a toothpick inserted in center comes out with moist crumbs (do not overbake).

4. Cool completely in pan on a wire rack. If desired, dust with confectioners' sugar. Cut into bars.

1 BROWNIE: 410 cal., 28g fat (12g sat. fat), 77mg chol., 186mg sod., 36g carb. (26g sugars, 3g fiber), 6g pro.

How to Cut Brownies

Give this trick a try when you want perfectly cut treats to take to the bake sale, potluck or party.

- Before pouring the batter, line the pan with parchment, letting a couple of inches extend over each side. Bake as directed. When brownies are cool, grab the paper handles and tug. The entire batch of brownies should come right out of the pan.

- A bench scraper (find one in the kitchenware aisle) is a handy tool for making clean cuts and/or working with dough. Get clean slices by firmly pressing the scraper into the brownies and lifting up rather than dragging it through the dessert.

Big & Buttery Chocolate Chip Cookies

Our version of the classic cookie is based on a recipe from a bakery in California called Hungry Bear. It's big, thick and chewy-perfect for dunking.
—*Irene Yeh, Mequon, WI*

PREP: 35 MIN. + CHILLING • BAKE: 10 MIN./BATCH • MAKES: ABOUT 2 DOZEN

1 cup butter, softened
1 cup packed brown sugar
¾ cup sugar
2 large eggs, room temperature
1½ tsp. vanilla extract
2⅔ cups all-purpose flour
1¼ tsp. baking soda
1 tsp. salt
1 pkg. (12 oz.) semisweet chocolate chips
2 cups coarsely chopped walnuts, toasted

READER REVIEW
"These are by far the best chocolate chip cookies I have ever made! They are our family's new favorite!"
—JOEY, TASTEOFHOME.COM

1. In a large bowl, beat butter and sugars until blended. Beat in eggs and vanilla. In a small bowl, whisk flour, baking soda and salt; gradually beat into butter mixture. Stir in chocolate chips and walnuts.

2. Shape ¼ cupfuls of dough into balls. Flatten each to ¾-in. thickness (2½-in. diameter), smoothing edges as necessary. Place in an airtight container, separating layers with waxed paper or parchment; refrigerate, covered, overnight.

3. To bake, place the dough portions 2 in. apart on parchment-lined baking sheets; let stand at room temperature 30 minutes before baking. Preheat oven to 400°.

4. Bake until edges are golden brown (centers will be light), 10-12 minutes. Cool on pans 2 minutes. Remove to wire racks to cool.

1 COOKIE: 311 cal., 19g fat (8g sat. fat), 38mg chol., 229mg sod., 35g carb. (23g sugars, 2g fiber), 4g pro.

Cranberry Chocolate Cookies with a Kick

Here's a chocolate cookie that makes you stop in your tracks to figure out what that surprising flavor is on the back of your palate.
—*Shalana Patout, Lafayette, LA*

PREP: 20 MIN. • **BAKE:** 10 MIN./BATCH • **MAKES:** 2 DOZEN

1 cup dried cranberries
¼ cup coffee liqueur or strong brewed coffee
1¼ cups semisweet chocolate chunks
¼ cup unsalted butter, cubed
2 large eggs, room temperature
¾ cup packed brown sugar
3 tsp. vanilla extract
1 cup all-purpose flour
½ tsp. baking powder
½ tsp. salt
½ tsp. ground cinnamon
½ tsp. freshly ground pepper
⅛ to ¼ tsp. cayenne pepper

1. Preheat oven to 350°. In a small saucepan, combine cranberries and liqueur. Bring just to a simmer; remove from the heat. In a microwave-safe bowl, microwave the chocolate and butter on high in 30-second intervals until melted; stir until smooth (the mixture will be thick). Cool slightly.

2. In a large bowl, beat eggs, brown sugar and vanilla on high until thickened, about 3 minutes; beat in chocolate mixture. In another bowl, whisk flour, baking powder, salt and seasonings; fold into sugar mixture just until combined. Fold in the cranberry mixture.

3. Drop by rounded tablespoonfuls 2 in. apart onto parchment-lined baking sheets. Bake 10-12 minutes or until cookies are shiny and tops are crackly. Cool on pans 2 minutes. Remove to wire racks to cool.

1 COOKIE: 146 cal., 5g fat (3g sat. fat), 21mg chol., 69mg sod., 24g carb. (18g sugars, 1g fiber), 2g pro.

Deep-Chocolate Zucchini Brownies

A fast-to-fix peanut butter and chocolate frosting tops these
cakelike brownies that are a sweet way to use up your garden bounty.
—*Allyson Wilkins, Amherst, NH*

PREP: 20 MIN. • BAKE: 35 MIN. • MAKES: 1½ DOZEN

1 cup butter, softened
1½ cups sugar
2 large eggs, room
  temperature
½ cup plain yogurt
1 tsp. vanilla extract
2½ cups all-purpose flour
¼ cup baking cocoa
1 tsp. baking soda
½ tsp. salt
2 cups shredded zucchini

FROSTING
⅔ cup semisweet
  chocolate chips
½ cup creamy
  peanut butter

1. Preheat oven to 350°. In a large bowl, cream butter and sugar until light and fluffy, 5-7 minutes. Add eggs, 1 at a time, beating well after each addition. Beat in yogurt and vanilla. In another bowl, combine flour, cocoa, baking soda and salt; gradually add to the creamed mixture. Stir in the zucchini.

2. Pour batter into a greased 13x9-in. baking pan. Bake until a toothpick inserted in the center comes out clean, 35-40 minutes.

3. For frosting, in a small saucepan, combine chocolate chips and peanut butter. Cook and stir over low heat until smooth. Spread over warm brownies. Cool on a wire rack. Cut into bars.

1 BROWNIE: 307 cal., 17g fat (8g sat. fat), 52mg chol., 283mg sod., 37g carb. (21g sugars, 2g fiber), 5g pro.

Chocolate Mint Dreams

My favorite flavor combo is chocolate and mint, so these frosted cookies are hard to resist. Luckily, I always manage to save some for friends.
—*Anne Revers, Omaha, NE*

PREP: 30 MIN. • **BAKE:** 5 MIN./BATCH + COOLING • **MAKES:** ABOUT 3 DOZEN

¾ cup butter, softened
½ cup confectioners' sugar
2 oz. unsweetened chocolate, melted and cooled
¼ tsp. peppermint extract
1½ cups all-purpose flour
1 cup miniature semisweet chocolate chips

ICING
2 Tbsp. butter, softened
1 cup confectioners' sugar
¼ tsp. peppermint extract
1 to 2 Tbsp. 2% milk
1 to 2 drops green food coloring, optional

DRIZZLE
½ cup semisweet chocolate chips
½ tsp. shortening

1. Preheat oven to 375°. Cream together butter and confectioners' sugar until light and fluffy, 5-7 minutes. Beat in cooled chocolate and extract. Gradually beat in flour. Stir in chocolate chips. (Dough will be soft.)

2. Drop the dough by tablespoonfuls 2 in. apart onto ungreased baking sheets. Bake until firm, 5-7 minutes. Cool on pans 2 minutes. Remove to wire racks to cool completely.

3. For icing, mix butter, confectioners' sugar, extract and enough milk to achieve desired consistency. If desired, tint green with food coloring. Spoon icing onto cookies.

4. In a microwave, melt chocolate chips and shortening; stir until smooth. Drizzle over tops.

1 COOKIE: 123 cal., 8g fat (5g sat. fat), 12mg chol., 37mg sod., 14g carb. (9g sugars, 1g fiber), 1g pro.

SWEET SECRET
If you use a fork dipped in melted chocolate for your drizzle, let the first clumpy drip land in the pan before you move the fork over to the cookies. Another option is to fill a heavy plastic storage bag with the melted chocolate, and snip off a small piece of 1 corner to use it as a pastry bag.

Chocolate Chip Brownies

People love these very rich brownies so much that I never take them anywhere without bringing along several copies of the recipe to hand out to friends.
—*Brenda Kelly, Ashburn, VA*

PREP: 10 MIN. • **BAKE:** 30 MIN. + COOLING • **MAKES:** 4 DOZEN

1   cup butter, softened
3   cups sugar
6   large eggs, room
    temperature
1   Tbsp. vanilla extract
2¼ cups all-purpose flour
½   cup baking cocoa
1   tsp. baking powder
½   tsp. salt
1   cup semisweet
    chocolate chips
1   cup vanilla or
    white chips
1   cup chopped walnuts

1. In a large bowl, cream butter and sugar until light and fluffy, 5-7 minutes. Add eggs and vanilla; mix well. Combine the flour, cocoa, baking powder and salt; gradually add to creamed mixture just until blended (do not overmix).

2. Pour into 2 greased 9-in. square baking pans. Sprinkle with chips and nuts. Bake at 350° until a toothpick inserted in the center comes out clean, 30-35 minutes. Cool.

1 BROWNIE: 167 cal., 8g fat (4g sat. fat), 38mg chol., 83mg sod., 22g carb. (14g sugars, 1g fiber), 3g pro.

NOTES

Chocolate Orange Rounds

To give a gift from the Sunshine State, I make these orange-flavored cookies and ship them to family and friends across the country.
—*Geordyth Sullivan, Cutler Bay, FL*

PREP: 40 MIN. + CHILLING • **BAKE:** 5 MIN./BATCH • **MAKES:** ABOUT 6½ DOZEN

1 cup butter, softened
1½ cups sugar
1 large egg, room temperature
1 tsp. orange extract
2½ cups all-purpose flour
1½ tsp. baking powder
¼ tsp. salt
2½ tsp. grated orange zest
2 oz. unsweetened chocolate, melted

1. In a large bowl, cream butter and sugar until light and fluffy, 5-7 minutes. Beat in egg and extract. In another bowl, whisk flour, baking powder and salt; gradually beat into creamed mixture. Divide dough in half. Add orange zest to 1 half; add melted chocolate to the other half.

2. Shape each portion into two 10x1-in. rolls. Wrap each and refrigerate 3 hours or overnight.

3. Preheat oven to 375°. Cut each roll down the center lengthwise. Reassemble rolls, alternating chocolate and orange halves. If necessary, wrap and chill until firm enough to slice.

4. Unwrap and cut into ¼-in. slices. Place 2 in. apart on ungreased baking sheets. Bake 5-6 minutes or until set. Remove from pans to wire racks to cool.

1 COOKIE: 54 cal., 3g fat (2g sat. fat), 9mg chol., 32mg sod., 7g carb. (4g sugars, 0 fiber), 1g pro. **DIABETIC EXCHANGES:** ½ starch.

NOTES

_____
_____
_____
_____
_____
_____
_____
_____
_____
_____

Crinkle-Top Chocolate Cookies

When I baked these moist, fudgy cookies for the first time, my three preschool children went wild over them! But I like them because they're lower in fat and easy to mix and bake.
—*Maria Groff, Ephrata, PA*

PREP: 15 MIN. + CHILLING • **BAKE:** 10 MIN./BATCH + COOLING • **MAKES:** ABOUT 3½ DOZEN

- 2 **cups semisweet chocolate chips, divided**
- 2 **Tbsp. butter, softened**
- 1 **cup sugar**
- 2 **large egg whites, room temperature**
- 1½ **tsp. vanilla extract**
- 1½ **cups all-purpose flour**
- 1½ **tsp. baking powder**
- ¼ **tsp. salt**
- ¼ **cup water**
- ½ **cup confectioners' sugar**

1. In a microwave, melt 1 cup chocolate chips. Stir until smooth; set aside. Beat butter and sugar until crumbly, about 2 minutes. Add egg whites and vanilla; beat well. Stir in melted chocolate.

2. In another bowl, whisk together flour, baking powder and salt; gradually add to butter mixture alternately with water. Stir in the remaining chocolate chips. Refrigerate, covered, until easy to handle, about 2 hours.

3. Preheat oven to 350°. Shape dough into 1-in. balls. Roll in confectioners' sugar. Place 2 in. apart on baking sheets coated with cooking spray. Bake until set, 10-12 minutes. Remove to wire racks to cool.

1 COOKIE: 85 cal., 3g fat (2g sat. fat), 1mg chol., 39mg sod., 15g carb. (11g sugars, 1g fiber), 1g pro. **DIABETIC EXCHANGES:** 1 starch, ½ fat.

READER REVIEW

"These 'yummies' are a definite favorite in my family. I also make oodles of them to give as Christmas gifts. They cannot be beat!"
—JOSCY, TASTEOFHOME.COM

Peanut Caramel Brownie Bites

With their three irresistible layers, these brownies are my family's absolute favorite.
—*Ella Agans, Birch Tree, MO*

PREP: 1 HOUR + CHILLING • **BAKE:** 20 MIN. + COOLING • **MAKES:** 4 DOZEN

¾ cup butter, cubed
  and softened
⅔ cup sugar
2 Tbsp. water
1 cup semisweet
  chocolate chips
2 large eggs, room
  temperature
1 tsp. vanilla extract
1 cup all-purpose flour
½ tsp. baking powder

TOPPING

1 cup sugar
¼ cup butter, cubed
¼ cup 2% milk
1 cup marshmallow
  creme
½ cup creamy peanut
  butter, divided
½ tsp. vanilla extract
2½ cups dry roasted
  peanuts, divided
40 caramels
2 Tbsp. water
1¼ cups semisweet
  chocolate chips

1. Preheat oven to 350°. Line a 13x9-in. baking pan with foil, letting the ends extend up sides; coat the foil with cooking spray.

2. Microwave butter, sugar and water on high just until mixture comes to a boil, 3-4 minutes; stir until blended. Stir in the chocolate chips until melted. Whisk in eggs, 1 at a time, stirring well after each addition. Whisk in vanilla. Stir in the flour and baking powder.

3. Spread into prepared pan. Bake until a toothpick inserted in center comes out clean, 18-20 minutes. Cool 30 minutes.

4. For topping, combine the sugar, butter and milk in a large saucepan; bring to a boil, stirring constantly, over medium heat. Boil 5 minutes, stirring frequently. Stir in marshmallow creme, ¼ cup peanut butter and vanilla; pour over brownies. Sprinkle with 2 cups peanuts.

5. In a small saucepan, combine caramels and water; cook, stirring, over medium-high heat until blended. Pour over the peanuts.

6. Microwave chocolate chips on high until softened, about 1 minute. Stir in remaining peanut butter until smooth; pour over caramel layer. Chop remaining peanuts; sprinkle on top. Refrigerate at least 1 hour.

7. Lifting with foil, remove brownies from pan. Cut into bars. Store in an airtight container in the refrigerator.

1 BROWNIE BITE: 212 cal., 12g fat (5g sat. fat), 19mg chol., 135mg sod., 24g carb. (19g sugars, 1g fiber), 4g pro.

Spiced Brownie Bites

My son and I came up with this recipe together to satisfy our cravings for chocolate and spice. What an enticing new way to enjoy chocolate!
—*Anna Nicoletta, East Stroudsburg, PA*

PREP: 40 MIN. • **BAKE:** 15 MIN. + COOLING • **MAKES:** ABOUT 3½ DOZEN

8 oz. bittersweet chocolate, coarsely chopped
½ cup butter, cubed
4 large eggs, room temperature
1 cup sugar
¾ cup packed brown sugar
1¼ cups all-purpose flour
⅓ cup baking cocoa
¾ tsp. cayenne pepper
¾ tsp. Chinese five-spice powder
½ tsp. salt

GLAZE
1 cup semisweet chocolate chips
4 Tbsp. butter, cubed
1 Tbsp. light corn syrup
Chopped crystallized ginger

1. Preheat oven to 350°. In a metal bowl or top of a double boiler over barely simmering water, melt chocolate and butter; stir until smooth. Cool slightly.

2. In a large bowl, beat eggs and sugars until blended; stir in chocolate mixture. In another bowl, mix flour, cocoa, spices and salt; gradually add to the chocolate mixture, mixing well.

3. Fill greased mini muffin cups almost full. Bake until centers are set, 12-15 minutes (do not overbake). Cool in pans 5 minutes before removing to wire racks to cool completely.

4. In a small metal bowl or top of a double boiler over barely simmering water, melt chocolate chips and butter with corn syrup, stirring until smooth. Remove from heat; cool until slightly thickened, about 30 minutes.

5. Dip tops of brownies into glaze. Top with ginger.

1 BROWNIE BITE: 137 cal., 7g fat (4g sat. fat), 26mg chol., 63mg sod., 16g carb. (12g sugars, 1g fiber), 2g pro.

Double Chocolate Almond Cheesecake

This cheesecake is easy—but it's definitely not easy to wait overnight to eat it!
If you're a chocolate lover, this is one dessert you have to try.
—*Darlene Brenden, Salem, OR*

PREP: 25 MIN. + CHILLING • BAKE: 50 MIN. + CHILLING • MAKES: 16 SERVINGS

CRUST
- 1   pkg. (9 oz.) chocolate wafer cookies, crushed (about 2 cups)
- ¼   cup sugar
- ¼   tsp. ground cinnamon
- ¼   cup butter, melted

FILLING
- 2   pkg. (8 oz. each) cream cheese, softened
- 1   cup sugar
- 1   cup sour cream
- 8   oz. semisweet chocolate, melted and cooled
- ½   tsp. almond extract
- 2   large eggs, room temperature, lightly beaten

TOPPING
- 1   cup sour cream
- ¼   tsp. baking cocoa
- 2   Tbsp. sugar
- ½   tsp. almond extract
  Sliced almonds, toasted, optional

1. In a small bowl, combine crust ingredients; reserve 2 Tbsp. for garnish. Press remaining crumbs evenly onto the bottom and 2 in. up the sides of a 9-in. springform pan. Chill.

2. For filling, in a large bowl, beat the cream cheese and sugar until smooth. Beat in the sour cream, chocolate and extract. Add eggs; beat on low speed just until combined. Pour into crust.

3. Place the pan on a baking sheet. Bake at 350° for 40 minutes (filling will not be set). Remove from oven and let stand for 5 minutes.

4. Meanwhile, combine the topping ingredients. Gently spread over the filling. Sprinkle with reserved crumbs. Bake 10 minutes longer.

5. Cool on a wire rack for 10 minutes. Carefully run a knife around edge of pan to loosen; cool 1 hour longer. Refrigerate overnight. Garnish with sliced, toasted almonds if desired.

1 SLICE: 315 cal., 19g fat (11g sat. fat), 78mg chol., 215mg sod., 31g carb. (19g sugars, 1g fiber), 4g pro.

Dark Chocolate Coconut Muffins

With a rich dark chocolate flavor and luscious cream cheese-coconut topping, these irresistible muffins taste more like a decadent dessert than a morning treat.
—*Sonia Daily, Rochester, MI*

PREP: 30 MIN. • BAKE: 20 MIN. •MAKES: 20 MUFFINS

4   oz. cream cheese,
    softened
3   Tbsp. sugar
2   Tbsp. all-purpose flour
1   large egg, room
    temperature
1   cup semisweet
    chocolate chips, divided
¾   cup sweetened
    shredded coconut
½   cup chopped pecans,
    toasted

BATTER
1½ cups all-purpose flour
1   cup packed brown
    sugar
¼   cup baking cocoa
1   tsp. baking soda
¼   tsp. ground cinnamon
1   cup brewed coffee,
    room temperature
⅓   cup canola oil
2   Tbsp. cider vinegar

1. Preheat oven to 350°. In a small bowl, beat cream cheese, sugar and flour until smooth. Beat in egg. Stir in ⅔ cup chocolate chips. In another bowl, toss coconut with pecans and remaining ⅓ cup chips.

2. In a large bowl, whisk together the first 5 batter ingredients. In another bowl, whisk together the coffee, oil and vinegar; add to the dry ingredients, stirring just until moistened.

3. Fill paper-lined muffin cups half full. Place scant 1 Tbsp. cream cheese mixture in the center of each. Top with about 1 Tbsp. coconut mixture.

4. Bake until a toothpick inserted in the center comes out clean, 20-25 minutes. Cool 5 minutes before removing from pans to wire racks to cool. Serve warm.

1 MUFFIN: 223 cal., 12g fat (4g sat. fat), 15mg chol., 98mg sod., 29g carb. (19g sugars, 1g fiber), 3g pro.

SWEET SECRET
Dress up mornings when you stir leftover coconut into pancake batter, sprinkle it over yogurt, mix it into oatmeal or add it to fruit medleys.

Chocolate Chip Pumpkin Bread

I love baking this bread in fall. The aroma is mouthwatering, and the chocolate chips add so much to an all-time favorite.
—*Vicki Raboine, Kansasville, WI*

PREP: 15 MIN. • **BAKE:** 45 MIN. • **MAKES:** 4 MINI LOAVES (6 SLICES EACH)

1 **cup packed brown sugar**
1 **cup sugar**
⅔ **cup butter, softened**
3 **large eggs, room temperature**
2⅓ **cups all-purpose flour**
1½ **cups canned pumpkin**
½ **cup water**
2 **tsp. baking soda**
1 **tsp. ground cinnamon**
1 **tsp. salt**
½ **tsp. ground cloves**
2 **cups semisweet chocolate chips**

1. In a bowl, cream sugars, butter and eggs. Add flour, pumpkin, water, baking soda, cinnamon, salt and cloves. Mix thoroughly. Fold in chocolate chips.

2. Pour into 4 greased and floured 5¾x3x2-in. loaf pans. Bake at 350° for 45 minutes or until breads test done.

1 SLICE: 239 cal., 10g fat (6g sat. fat), 37mg chol., 258mg sod., 37g carb. (26g sugars, 2g fiber), 3g pro.

NOTES

_____
_____
_____
_____
_____
_____
_____

Triple-Chocolate Cream Puffs

Here's a triple treat for chocolate fans: chocolate cream puffs with a rich, velvety chocolate-orange filling that's topped with a homemade chocolate syrup. Yum!
—*Agnes Ward, Stratford, ON*

PREP: 35 MIN. • **BAKE:** 20 MIN. + COOLING • **MAKES:** 2 DOZEN

1   **cup water**
½   **cup butter, cubed**
1   **oz. semisweet chocolate, chopped**
¼   **tsp. salt**
1   **cup all-purpose flour**
4   **large eggs, room temperature**

CHOCOLATE ORANGE FILLING
2   **cups semisweet chocolate chips**
⅔   **cup reduced-fat evaporated milk**
2   **Tbsp. orange marmalade**
2   **Tbsp. orange liqueur**
4   **cups whipped topping**

CHOCOLATE SYRUP
½   **cup sugar**
¼   **cup baking cocoa**
1   **Tbsp. cornstarch Dash salt**
1   **cup water**
1   **tsp. vanilla extract**

1. In a large saucepan, bring water, butter, chocolate and salt to a boil. Add flour all at once and stir until a smooth ball forms. Remove from the heat; let stand for 5 minutes. Add eggs, 1 at a time, beating well after each addition. Continue beating until mixture is smooth and shiny.

2. Drop by tablespoonfuls 2 in. apart onto greased baking sheets. Bake at 400° for 20-25 minutes or until set. Pierce side of each puff with tip of knife. Cool on wire racks. Split puffs open. Pull out and discard soft dough from inside tops and bottoms.

3. For filling, in a small saucepan, combine the chocolate chips, milk and marmalade. Cook and stir until chips are melted. Cool to room temperature. Stir in orange liqueur; fold in whipped topping. Refrigerate until ready to use.

4. For syrup, in a small saucepan, combine the sugar, cocoa, cornstarch and salt. Stir in water until blended. Bring to a boil; cook and stir for 2 minutes or until thickened. Remove from the heat; stir in vanilla. Cool to room temperature.

5. Just before serving, fill cream puffs with filling; drizzle with chocolate syrup.

1 CREAM PUFF: 206 cal., 11g fat (7g sat. fat), 46mg chol., 80mg sod., 24g carb. (16g sugars, 1g fiber), 3g pro.

S'mores Monkey Bread Muffins

Kids of all ages love these ooey-gooey individual-sized monkey breads.
Made with frozen dinner rolls, they simply couldn't be easier to prepare.
—*Tina Butler, Royse City, TX*

PREP: 35 MIN. • BAKE: 15 MIN. • MAKES: 1 DOZEN

15 **frozen bread dough dinner rolls, thawed but still cold**
1⅓ **cups graham cracker crumbs**
½ **cup sugar**
6 **Tbsp. butter, cubed**
1 **cup miniature semisweet chocolate chips, divided**
¾ **cup miniature marshmallows**

ICING
1 **cup confectioners' sugar**
½ **tsp. butter, softened**
1 **to 2 Tbsp. 2% milk**

SWEET SECRET
Jazz up these muffins with dried fruit. Add dried cranberries to the crumb-covered dough in the muffin cups for a nice burst of flavor, color and even texture.

1. Preheat oven to 375°. Line 12 muffin cups with foil liners.

2. Using a sharp knife, cut each dinner roll into 4 pieces. In a shallow bowl, mix cracker crumbs and sugar. In a large microwave-safe bowl, microwave butter until melted. Dip 3 pieces of dough in butter, then roll in crumb mixture to coat; place in a prepared muffin cup. Repeat until all muffin cups are filled. Sprinkle tops with ¾ cup chocolate chips and the marshmallows.

3. Toss remaining dough pieces with remaining butter, rewarming butter if necessary. Place 2 additional dough pieces in each cup; sprinkle with the remaining chocolate chips.

4. Bake until golden brown, 15-20 minutes. Cool 5 minutes before removing from pan to a wire rack. Mix the icing ingredients; spoon over tops. Serve warm.

1 MUFFIN: 351 cal., 13g fat (6g sat. fat), 16mg chol., 337mg sod., 57g carb. (29g sugars, 3g fiber), 6g pro.

Classic Long Johns

I came across the recipe for these wonderful treats years ago. I remember Mom making something similar to these. You can frost them with maple or chocolate glaze.
—*Ann Sorgent, Fond du Lac, WI*

PREP: 30 MIN. + RISING • **COOK:** 5 MIN./BATCH + COOLING • **MAKES:** 2 DOZEN

2 pkg. (¼ oz. each) active dry yeast
½ cup warm water (110° to 115°)
½ cup half-and-half cream
¼ cup sugar
¼ cup shortening
1 large egg, room temperature
1 tsp. salt
½ tsp. ground nutmeg
3 to 3½ cups all-purpose flour
   Oil for deep-fat frying

MAPLE FROSTING
¼ cup packed brown sugar
2 Tbsp. butter
1 Tbsp. half-and-half cream
⅛ tsp. maple flavoring
½ cup confectioners' sugar

CHOCOLATE FROSTING
2 oz. semisweet chocolate, chopped
2 Tbsp. butter
½ cup confectioners' sugar
2 Tbsp. boiling water
1 tsp. vanilla extract

1. In a large bowl, dissolve yeast in warm water. Add cream, sugar, shortening, egg, salt, nutmeg and 3 cups flour. Beat until smooth. Stir in enough remaining flour to form a soft dough (dough will be sticky).

2. Turn onto a floured surface; knead until smooth and elastic, 6-8 minutes. Place in a greased bowl, turning once to grease the top. Cover and let rise in a warm place until doubled, about 1 hour.

3. Punch down dough; divide in half. Turn onto a lightly floured surface; roll each half into a 12x6-in. rectangle. Cut each portion into twelve 3x2-in. rectangles. Place on greased baking sheets. Cover and let rise in a warm place until doubled, about 30 minutes.

4. In an electric skillet or deep fryer, heat oil to 375°. Fry long johns, a few at a time, until golden brown on both sides. Drain on paper towels.

5. For maple frosting, combine brown sugar and butter in a small saucepan. Bring to a boil, stirring to dissolve sugar. Remove from heat; stir in cream and maple flavoring. Add the confectioners' sugar; beat for 1 minute or until smooth. Frost cooled long johns.

6. For chocolate frosting, in a microwave, melt chocolate and butter; stir until smooth. Stir in remaining ingredients. Spread over cooled long johns; let stand until set.

1 LONG JOHN: 186 cal., 9g fat (3g sat. fat), 16mg chol., 121mg sod., 22g carb. (10g sugars, 1g fiber), 3g pro.

Chocolate Pinwheel Bread

This swirled yeast bread is chock-full of chocolate chips. The sweet slices don't need any butter. Keep one loaf and share the other with a neighbor.
—*Dawn Onuffer, Crestview, FL*

PREP: 30 MIN. + RISING • **BAKE:** 40 MIN. + COOLING • **MAKES:** 2 LOAVES (16 SLICES EACH)

1 **pkg. (¼ oz.) active dry yeast**
1 **cup warm whole milk (110° to 115°)**
¼ **cup sugar**
1 **tsp. salt**
2 **large eggs, room temperature**
4 **oz. cream cheese, softened**
4 **to 4½ cups bread flour**

FILLING
4 **oz. cream cheese, softened**
½ **cup confectioners' sugar**
2 **Tbsp. baking cocoa**
1 **cup semisweet chocolate chips**
1 **large egg, beaten**

1. In a large bowl, dissolve yeast in warm milk. Add the sugar, salt, eggs, cream cheese and 2 cups flour; beat until smooth. Stir in enough remaining flour to form a soft dough.

2. Turn onto a floured surface; knead until smooth and elastic, 6-8 minutes. Place in a greased bowl, turning once to grease top. Cover and let rise in a warm place until doubled, about 1 hour.

3. Punch dough down. Turn onto a floured surface; divide in half. Roll each portion into a 12x8-in. rectangle. For the filling, in a small bowl, beat cream cheese, confectioners' sugar and cocoa until smooth. Spread over each rectangle to within ½ in. of edges. Sprinkle with chocolate chips. Roll up jelly-roll style, starting with a short side; pinch seam to seal. Place seam side down in 2 greased 9x5-in. loaf pans. Cover and let rise until doubled, about 45 minutes. Preheat oven to 350°.

4. Brush tops of loaves with egg. Bake 25 minutes; cover loosely with foil. Bake 15-20 minutes longer or until loaves sound hollow when tapped. Remove from pans to wire racks to cool.

1 SLICE: 127 cal., 5g fat (3g sat. fat), 29mg chol., 105mg sod., 19g carb. (7g sugars, 1g fiber), 4g pro.

Chocolate Eclairs

With creamy filling and thick decadent frosting, these eclairs are extra special.
Now you can indulge in classic treats without leaving the house!
—*Jessica Campbell, Viola, WI*

PREP: 45 MIN. • **BAKE:** 35 MIN. + COOLING • **MAKES:** 9 SERVINGS

1   **cup water**
½   **cup butter, cubed**
¼   **tsp. salt**
1   **cup all-purpose flour**
4   **large eggs, room
    temperature**

FILLING
2½ **cups cold whole milk**
1   **pkg. (5.1 oz.) instant
    vanilla pudding mix**
1   **cup heavy
    whipping cream**
¼   **cup confectioners'
    sugar**
1   **tsp. vanilla extract**

FROSTING
2   **oz. semisweet
    chocolate**
2   **Tbsp. butter**
1¼ **cups confectioners'
    sugar**
2   **to 3 Tbsp. hot water**

1. Preheat oven to 400°. In a large saucepan, bring water, butter and salt to a boil. Add flour all at once and stir until a smooth ball forms. Remove from heat; let stand 5 minutes. Add eggs, 1 at a time, beating well after each addition. Continue beating until the mixture is smooth and shiny.

2. Using a tablespoon or a pastry tube with a #10 or large round tip, form the dough into nine 4x1½-in. strips on a greased baking sheet. Bake 35-40 minutes or until puffed and golden. Remove to a wire rack. Immediately split eclairs open; remove tops and set aside. Discard soft dough from inside. Cool eclairs.

3. For filling, in a large bowl, beat milk and pudding mix according to package directions. In another bowl, whip cream until soft peaks form. Beat in sugar and vanilla; fold into pudding. Fill eclairs (chill any remaining filling for another use).

4. For frosting, in a microwave, melt chocolate and butter; stir until smooth. Stir in sugar and enough hot water to achieve a smooth consistency. Cool slightly. Frost the eclairs. Store in refrigerator.

1 ECLAIR: 483 cal., 28g fat (17g sat. fat), 174mg chol., 492mg sod., 52g carb. (37g sugars, 1g fiber), 7g pro.

Delicious Potato Doughnuts

I first tried these treats at my sister's house and thought they were the best I'd ever had. They're easy to make, and the fudge frosting tops them off well.
—*Pat Davis, Beulah, MI*

PREP: 20 MIN. • **COOK:** 40 MIN. • **MAKES:** 4 DOZEN

2 **cups hot mashed potatoes (with added milk and butter)**
2½ **cups sugar**
2 **cups buttermilk**
2 **large eggs, lightly beaten**
2 **Tbsp. butter, melted**
2 **tsp. baking soda**
2 **tsp. baking powder**
1 **tsp. salt**
1 **tsp. ground nutmeg**
6½ to 7 **cups all-purpose flour**
   Oil for deep-fat frying

FAST FUDGE FROSTING
3¾ **cups confectioners' sugar**
½ **cup baking cocoa**
¼ **tsp. salt**
⅓ **cup boiling water**
⅓ **cup butter, melted**
1 **tsp. vanilla extract**

1. In a large bowl, combine the potatoes, sugar, buttermilk and eggs. Stir in the butter, baking soda, baking powder, salt, nutmeg and enough of the flour to form a soft dough. Turn onto a lightly floured surface; pat out to ¾-in. thickness. Cut with a 2½-in. floured doughnut cutter.

2. In an electric skillet, heat 1 in. of oil to 375°. Fry the doughnuts for 2 minutes on each side or until browned. Place on paper towels.

3. For frosting, combine the confectioners' sugar, cocoa and salt in a large bowl. Stir in the water, butter and vanilla. Dip tops of warm doughnuts in frosting.

1 DOUGHNUT: 226 cal., 9g fat (2g sat. fat), 15mg chol., 185mg sod., 35g carb. (20g sugars, 1g fiber), 3g pro.

READER REVIEW
"I made these doughnuts years ago, and they are fabulous! They also make a huge batch. They are very tasty. I will make again for sure! Great recipe!"
—LLABMIK, TASTEOFHOME.COM

Chocolate Babka

I love this chocolate babka. It's a rewarding recipe for taking the next step in your bread baking. Even if it's slightly imperfect going into the oven, it turns out gorgeous.
—*Lisa Kaminski, Wauwatosa, WI*

PREP: 20 MIN. + CHILLING • **BAKE:** 35 MIN. + COOLING • **MAKES:** 2 LOAVES (16 SLICES EACH)

4¼ to 4¾ cups all-purpose flour
½ cup sugar
2½ tsp. quick-rise yeast
¾ tsp. salt
⅔ cup butter
½ cup water
3 large eggs plus 1 large egg yolk, room temperature, beaten
2 Tbsp. grated orange zest

FILLING
½ cup butter, cubed
5 oz. dark chocolate chips
½ cup confectioners' sugar
⅓ cup baking cocoa
¼ tsp. salt

GLAZE
¼ cup sugar
¼ cup water

1. In a large bowl, mix 2 cups flour, sugar, yeast and salt. Cut in butter until crumbly. In a small saucepan, heat water to 120°-130°; stir into dry ingredients. Stir in eggs and yolk, orange zest and enough remaining flour to form a soft dough (dough will be sticky).

2. Turn dough onto a floured surface; knead until smooth and elastic, 6-8 minutes. Place in a greased bowl, turning once to grease the top. Cover and refrigerate for 8 hours or overnight.

3. Turn out dough onto a lightly floured surface; divide in half. Roll each half into a 12x10-in. rectangle. For filling, in a microwave, melt butter and chocolate chips; stir until smooth. Stir in confectioners' sugar, cocoa and salt. Spread filling to within ½ in. of edges. Roll up jelly-roll style, starting with a long side; pinch seam and ends to seal.

4. Using a sharp knife, cut each roll lengthwise in half; carefully turn each half cut side up. Loosely twist strips around each other, keeping cut surfaces facing up; pinch ends together to seal. Place in 2 greased 9x5-in. loaf pans, cut side up. Cover with kitchen towels; let rise in a warm place until almost doubled, about 1 hour. Preheat the oven to 375°.

5. Bake until golden brown, 35-45 minutes, tenting with foil halfway through. Meanwhile, in a saucepan, combine sugar and water; bring to a boil. Reduce heat; simmer, uncovered, 10 minutes. Brush over warm babka. Cool 10 minutes before removing from pans to wire racks.

1 SLICE: 181 cal., 9g fat (5g sat. fat), 41mg chol., 136mg sod., 23g carb. (10g sugars, 1g fiber), 3g pro.

Chocolate Cinnamon Rolls with Icing

Check these out! What a scrumptious change of pace from ordinary cinnamon rolls, and a perfect addition to coffee breaks. Serve them at brunch, too.

—Rita Lempka, Sterling, NE

PREP: 30 MIN. + RISING • **BAKE:** 25 MIN. • **MAKES:** 1 DOZEN

1 pkg. (¼ oz.) active dry yeast
¾ cup warm water (110° to 115°)
¼ cup shortening
1 tsp. salt
¼ cup plus 3 Tbsp. sugar, divided
1 large egg, room temperature
⅓ cup baking cocoa
2¼ cups all-purpose flour
1 Tbsp. butter, softened
1½ tsp. ground cinnamon

QUICK WHITE ICING
1 cup confectioners' sugar
½ tsp. vanilla extract
1½ Tbsp. whole milk

1. In a large bowl, dissolve yeast in warm water; let stand for 5 minutes. Add shortening, salt, ¼ cup sugar, egg, cocoa and 1 cup flour; beat for 2 minutes. Stir in remaining flour and blend with a spoon until smooth. Cover and let rise in a warm place until doubled, about 1 hour. Stir dough down and turn onto a well-floured surface (dough will be soft). Roll out into a 12x9-in. rectangle. Carefully spread with butter.

2. Combine cinnamon and remaining 3 Tbsp. sugar; sprinkle over butter. Roll up gently, beginning at a wide end. Cut into 12 pieces and place in a greased 9-in. square baking pan. Cover and let rise in a warm place until doubled, about 45 minutes. Bake at 375° for 25 minutes.

3. Meanwhile, for icing, stir all ingredients together in a small bowl until mixture is desired spreading consistency. Drizzle icing onto warm rolls.

1 CINNAMON ROLL: 214 cal., 6g fat (2g sat. fat), 21mg chol., 214mg sod., 37g carb. (17g sugars, 1g fiber), 4g pro.

3 Ways to Soften Butter

Did you forget to take the butter out early? No problem!

- SLICE IT! Cut the butter lengthwise. Stack and slice lengthwise again. Re-stack; slice butter crosswise to make cubes. The cubes will soften in about 15 minutes.

- ROLL IT! Place the butter between 2 sheets of waxed paper. Use a rolling pin to roll the butter flat.

- GRATE IT! Partially unwrap the butter (use the wrapped half as a handle), and shred it using the largest holes of a box grater.

Chocolate Quick Bread

My husband and I both enjoy cooking, but the baking is left to me. Our sons loved this chocolaty quick bread when they were little—and they still do as grownups!
—*Melissa Mitchell-Wilson, Wichita, KS*

PREP: 20 MIN. • **BAKE:** 55 MIN. + COOLING • **MAKES:** 1 LOAF (16 SLICES)

1¾ cups all-purpose flour
½ cup baking cocoa
½ tsp. baking powder
½ tsp. baking soda
½ tsp. salt
½ cup butter, softened
1 cup sugar
2 large eggs, room temperature
1 cup buttermilk
½ cup miniature semisweet chocolate chips
⅓ cup chopped pecans

1. In a large bowl, combine the flour, cocoa, baking powder, baking soda and salt. In a large bowl, cream butter and sugar until light and fluffy, 5-7 minutes. Add eggs, 1 at a time, beating well after each addition. Add buttermilk; mix well. Stir into dry ingredients just until moistened. Fold in chocolate chips and pecans.

2. Pour into a greased 9x5-in. loaf pan. Bake at 350° for 55-60 minutes or until a toothpick inserted in the center comes out clean. Cool for 10 minutes before removing from pan to a wire rack to cool completely.

1 SLICE. 214 cal., 10g fat (5g sat. fat), 42mg chol., 192mg sod., 29g carb. (17g sugars, 1g fiber), 4g pro.

Candy Bar Croissants

These croissants taste as good as they look. The rich, buttery treat combines convenient refrigerated crescent rolls and chocolate bars.
—*Beverly Coyde, Gasport, NY*

PREP: 15 MIN. • **BAKE:** 15 MIN. + COOLING • **MAKES:** 8 SERVINGS

1 tube (8 oz.) refrigerated crescent rolls
1 Tbsp. butter, softened
2 plain milk chocolate candy bars (1.55 oz. each), broken into small pieces
1 large egg, lightly beaten
2 Tbsp. sliced almonds

1. Unroll crescent roll dough; separate into triangles. Brush with butter. Arrange candy bar pieces evenly over triangles; roll up from the wide end.

2. Place point side down on a greased baking sheet; curve ends slightly. Brush with egg and sprinkle with almonds. Bake at 375° for 11-13 minutes or until golden brown. Cool on a wire rack.

1 CROISSANT: 170 cal., 11g fat (4g sat. fat), 32mg chol., 250mg sod., 15g carb. (5g sugars, 0 fiber), 4g pro.

Chocolate Chip Coffee Cake

With lots of chocolate and cinnamon appeal, this special breakfast treat never fails to please. What a lovely addition to morning coffee, and it's particularly good with a glass of cold milk.
—*Trish Quinn, Middletown, PA*

PREP: 10 MIN. • **BAKE:** 25 MIN. + COOLING • **MAKES:** 16 SERVINGS

½ cup butter, softened
1½ cups sugar, divided
2 large eggs, room
temperature
1 cup sour cream
1 tsp. vanilla extract
2½ cups all-purpose flour
1½ tsp. baking powder
1 tsp. baking soda
1 cup semisweet
chocolate chips
1 tsp. ground cinnamon

1. In a large bowl, cream butter and 1 cup sugar until light and fluffy. Add eggs, sour cream and vanilla; mix well. In another bowl, combine the flour, baking powder and baking soda; add to creamed mixture (batter will be thick).

2. Spread half of the batter into a greased 13x9-in. baking pan. Combine chocolate chips, cinnamon and remaining sugar; sprinkle half over batter. Drop remaining batter by spoonfuls over the top. Sprinkle with the remaining chip mixture. Bake at 350° for 25-30 minutes or until a toothpick inserted in the center comes out clean. Cool on a wire rack.

1 PIECE: 284 cal., 12g fat (7g sat. fat), 52mg chol., 191mg sod., 41g carb. (25g sugars, 1g fiber), 4g pro.

NOTES

_____
_____
_____
_____
_____
_____
_____
_____

Three-Layer Chocolate Ganache Cake

This decadent triple-layer beauty is pure chocolate indulgence.
—*Kathleen Smith, Overland, MO*

PREP: 30 MIN. • **BAKE:** 30 MIN. + CHILLING • **MAKES:** 16 SERVINGS

4 cups all-purpose flour
2¼ cups sugar
¾ cup baking cocoa
4 tsp. baking soda
2¼ cups mayonnaise
2¼ cups brewed coffee, cold
1½ tsp. vanilla extract

FILLING
1 cup sugar
2 Tbsp. cornstarch
1 cup 2% milk
2 tsp. vanilla extract
1 cup butter, softened
¾ cup miniature semisweet chocolate chips

GANACHE
8 oz. semisweet chocolate, chopped
2 cups heavy whipping cream
1 tsp. vanilla extract

GLAZE
8 oz. semisweet chocolate, chopped
¾ cup heavy whipping cream
¼ cup butter, cubed

1. Preheat oven to 350°. Line bottoms of 3 greased 9-in. round baking pans with parchment; grease paper. In a large bowl, whisk flour, sugar, cocoa and baking soda. Beat in mayonnaise, coffee and vanilla. Transfer batter to prepared pans. Bake 30-35 minutes or until a toothpick inserted in center comes out clean. Cool in the pans for 10 minutes before removing to wire racks; remove paper. Cool completely.

2. For filling, in a small heavy saucepan, mix sugar and cornstarch. Whisk in milk. Cook and stir over medium heat until thickened and bubbly. Reduce heat to low; cook and stir 2 minutes longer. Remove from heat; stir in vanilla. Cool completely. In a large bowl, cream butter. Gradually beat in cooled mixture. Stir in the chocolate chips.

3. For ganache, place chocolate in a large bowl. In a small saucepan, bring cream just to a boil. Pour over chocolate; let stand 5 minutes. Stir with a whisk until smooth. Stir in vanilla. Cool to room temperature, stirring occasionally. Refrigerate, covered, until cold. Beat ganache just until soft peaks form, 15-30 seconds (do not overbeat).

4. Place 1 cake layer on a serving plate; spread with half of the filling. Repeat layers. Top with the remaining cake layer. Frost top and sides of the cake with ganache. In a microwave-safe bowl, combine chocolate, cream and butter. Microwave at 50% power for 1-2 minutes or until smooth, stirring twice. Cool slightly, stirring occasionally. Drizzle over cake, allowing some to flow over the sides. Refrigerate at least 2 hours before serving.

1 SLICE: 970 cal., 65g fat (30g sat. fat), 88mg chol., 607mg sod., 81g carb. (53g sugars, 3g fiber), 8g pro.

Chocolate S'mores Tart

I created this tart for my kids, who love having s'mores on the fire pit. It's truly indulgent. We simply can't get enough of the impressive billowy marshmallow topping.
—*Dina Crowell, Fredericksburg, VA*

PREP: 30 MIN. + CHILLING • **MAKES:** 16 SERVINGS

1½ cups graham cracker
    crumbs
¼ cup sugar
⅓ cup butter, melted

FILLING
10 oz. bittersweet
    chocolate, chopped
¼ cup butter, cubed
1½ cups heavy
    whipping cream

TOPPING
5 large egg whites
1 cup sugar
¼ tsp. cream of tartar

1. In a small bowl, mix cracker crumbs and sugar; stir in butter. Press onto the bottom and ½ in. up the sides of an ungreased 9-in. fluted tart pan with removable bottom. Refrigerate 30 minutes.

2. Place chocolate and butter in a large bowl. In a small saucepan, bring cream just to a boil. Pour over chocolate and butter; let stand 5 minutes. Stir with a whisk until smooth. Pour into prepared tart shell. Refrigerate 1 hour or until set. Place egg whites in a large bowl; let stand at room temperature for 30 minutes.

3. In the top of a double boiler or in a metal bowl over simmering water, combine egg whites, sugar and cream of tartar. Beat on low speed 1 minute. Continue beating on low until a thermometer reads 160°, about 5 minutes longer. Transfer to a large bowl; beat on high until stiff glossy peaks form and mixture is slightly cooled, about 5 minutes.

4. Spread meringue over tart. If desired, heat meringue with a kitchen torch or broil 2 in. from heat until meringue is lightly browned, 30-45 seconds. Refrigerate leftovers.

1 SLICE: 332 cal., 24g fat (13g sat. fat), 49mg chol., 122mg sod., 33g carb. (25g sugars, 2g fiber), 4g pro.

SWEET SECRET
For a firmer crust, bake unfilled crust at 350° until lightly browned, 10-12 minutes. Cool on a wire rack.

Dream Cupcakes

My grandchildren absolutely love these cream-filled cupcakes,
and I hope the chocolaty treats become a favorite in your home as well.
—*Dorothy Bahlmann, Clarksville, IA*

PREP: 20 MIN. • BAKE: 25 MIN. • MAKES: 2½ DOZEN

1 pkg. chocolate cake mix (regular size)
6 oz. cream cheese, softened
⅓ cup sugar
1 large egg, room temperature
⅛ tsp. salt
1 cup semisweet chocolate chips
¼ cup sweetened shredded coconut, optional

1. Prepare cake mix according to package directions for cupcakes. Fill 30 paper-lined muffin cups half full. In a large bowl, beat cream cheese and sugar until fluffy. Beat in egg and salt until smooth. Stir in chocolate chips and, if desired, coconut.

2. Drop about 2 tsp. cream cheese mixture into the center of each cupcake. Bake at 350° until cake springs back when lightly touched, 25-30 minutes. Cool 5 minutes before removing from pans to wire racks. Store cupcakes in the refrigerator.

1 CUPCAKE: 155 cal., 8g fat (3g sat. fat), 34mg chol., 153mg sod., 20g carb. (14g sugars, 1g fiber), 2g pro. **DIABETIC EXCHANGES:** 1½ fat, 1 starch.

NOTES

_____
_____
_____
_____
_____
_____

Deep & Dark Ganache Cake

This is my ode to all things chocolate. Each layer of this coffee-spiked cake is smothered in silky ganache for a phenomenally rich and satisfying dessert.
—*Tarra Knight, Benbrook, TX*

PREP: 40 MIN. + COOLING • **BAKE:** 30 MIN. + COOLING • **MAKES:** 24 SERVINGS

- 6 **oz. bittersweet chocolate, chopped**
- 1½ **cups hot brewed coffee**
- 4 **large eggs**
- 3 **cups sugar**
- ¾ **cup canola oil**
- 2 **tsp. vanilla extract**
- 2½ **cups all-purpose flour**
- 1 **cup baking cocoa**
- 2 **tsp. baking soda**
- ¾ **tsp. baking powder**
- 1¼ **tsp. salt**
- 1½ **cups buttermilk**

GANACHE FROSTING

- 16 **oz. bittersweet chocolate, chopped**
- 2 **cups heavy whipping cream**
- 5 **tsp. light corn syrup**

1. Preheat oven to 325°. Line bottoms of 3 greased 8-in. square baking pans with parchment; grease the paper.

2. Place chocolate in a small bowl. Pour hot coffee over chocolate; stir with a whisk until smooth. Cool slightly.

3. In a large bowl, beat eggs on high speed until lemon-colored. Gradually add sugar, oil, vanilla and the chocolate mixture, beating until well blended. In another bowl, mix flour, cocoa, baking soda, baking powder and salt; add to chocolate mixture alternately with buttermilk, beating well after each addition.

4. Transfer to the prepared pans. Bake 30-35 minutes or until a toothpick inserted in center comes out clean. Cool 10 minutes before removing from pans to wire racks; remove paper. Cool completely.

5. For ganache, place chocolate in a large bowl. In a small saucepan, bring cream and corn syrup just to a boil. Pour over chocolate; stir with a whisk until smooth.

6. Let stand at room temperature to cool and thicken slightly, about 45 minutes, stirring occasionally. (Mixture will be very soft, but will thicken when spread onto cake.)

7. Place 1 cake layer on a serving plate; spread with ⅓ cup ganache. Repeat layers. Top with remaining cake layer. Spread remaining ganache over top and sides of the cake.

1 SLICE: 437 cal., 27g fat (11g sat. fat), 63mg chol., 277mg sod., 52g carb. (36g sugars, 3g fiber), 6g pro.

Chocolate-Glazed Cupcakes

Because I have a dairy allergy, I'm always on the search for treats I can eat. I prepare these cupcakes with dairy-free chocolate chips and vanilla coconut milk instead of cream.
—*Kirstin Turner, Richlands, NC*

PREP: 25 MIN. • **BAKE:** 15 MIN. + COOLING • **MAKES:** 16 CUPCAKES

1½ cups all-purpose flour
¾ cup sugar
⅓ cup baking cocoa
1 tsp. baking soda
¾ tsp. salt
1 cup water
¼ cup unsweetened applesauce
¼ cup canola oil
1 Tbsp. white vinegar
1 tsp. vanilla extract
⅔ cup semisweet chocolate chips, optional

GLAZE
½ cup semisweet chocolate chips
¼ cup half-and-half cream
White nonpareils, optional

1. Preheat the oven to 350°. Line 16 muffin cups with foil liners.

2. In a large bowl, whisk the first 5 ingredients. In another bowl, whisk water, applesauce, oil, vinegar and vanilla until blended. Add to flour mixture; stir just until moistened. If desired, stir in chocolate chips.

3. Fill prepared muffin cups three-fourths full. Bake until a toothpick inserted in center comes out clean, 14-16 minutes. Cool 5 minutes before removing from pans to wire racks; cool completely.

4. For glaze, in a small saucepan, combine chocolate chips and cream; cook and stir over low heat until smooth, 3-5 minutes. Remove from heat. Cool at room temperature until glaze is slightly thickened, stirring occasionally, about 30 minutes. Dip tops of cupcakes into glaze. If desired, sprinkle with nonpareils.

1 CUPCAKE: 148 cal., 6g fat (1g sat. fat), 2mg chol., 192mg sod., 23g carb. (13g sugars, 1g fiber), 2g pro. **DIABETIC EXCHANGES:** 1½ starch, 1 fat.

SWEET SECRET
Mix things up by replacing the vanilla extract with butter rum flavoring or almond or rum extract.

Chocolate Carrot Cake

Finely shredding the carrots gives this cake an extra-nice texture.
The walnuts sprinkled on top add crunch, but you can leave them off if you prefer.
—*Pamela Brown, Williamsburg, MI*

PREP: 35 MIN. • **BAKE:** 25 MIN. + COOLING • **MAKES:** 16 SERVINGS

3 **cups finely shredded carrots**
2 **cups sugar**
1¼ **cups canola oil**
4 **large eggs, room temperature**
2 **cups all-purpose flour**
½ **cup baking cocoa**
1 **tsp. baking soda**
½ **tsp. salt**

FROSTING
1 **pkg. (8 oz.) cream cheese, softened**
½ **cup butter, softened**
3¾ **cups confectioners' sugar**
¼ **cup baking cocoa**
3 **tsp. vanilla extract**
¼ **cup chopped walnuts**
¼ **cup semisweet chocolate chips**

1. Line two 9-in. round baking pans with waxed paper; grease the paper and set aside. In a large bowl, beat the carrots, sugar, oil and eggs until well blended. Combine the flour, cocoa, baking soda and salt; gradually beat into carrot mixture until blended.

2. Pour into prepared pans. Bake at 350° for 25-30 minutes or until a toothpick inserted in the center comes out clean. Cool for 10 minutes before removing from pans to wire racks to cool completely.

3. For frosting, in a large bowl, beat cream cheese and butter until fluffy. Beat in the confectioners' sugar, cocoa and vanilla until smooth.

4. Place bottom layer on a serving plate; top with half of the frosting. Repeat with remaining cake layer. Sprinkle with nuts and chocolate chips.

1 SLICE: 578 cal., 31g fat (10g sat. fat), 84mg chol., 276mg sod., 72g carb. (54g sugars, 2g fiber), 6g pro.

Orange Chocolate Ricotta Pie

A traditional Italian dessert served during the holidays and for special occasions, this pie features the classic pairing of orange and chocolate flavors. The result is rich and tangy. It's a perfect finale to a Mediterranean-style dinner.
—*Trisha Kruse, Eagle, ID*

PREP: 20 MIN. • **BAKE:** 40 MIN. + COOLING • **MAKES:** 8 SERVINGS

- 2 **cartons (15 oz. each) whole-milk ricotta cheese**
- 2 **large eggs, lightly beaten**
- ½ **cup dark chocolate chips**
- ⅓ **cup sugar**
- 1 **Tbsp. grated orange zest**
- 2 **Tbsp. orange liqueur, optional**
  Pastry for double-crust pie

1. In a large bowl, combine the ricotta cheese, eggs, chocolate chips, sugar, orange zest and, if desired, orange liqueur.

2. On a floured surface, roll out half the dough to fit a 9-in. pie plate; transfer to pie plate. Fill with ricotta mixture.

3. Roll out remaining dough into an 11-in. circle; cut into 1-in.-wide strips. Lay half of the strips across the pie, about 1 in. apart. Fold back every other strip halfway. Lay another strip across center of pie at a right angle. Unfold strips over center strip. Fold back the alternate strips; place a second strip across the pie. Continue to add strips until pie is covered with lattice. Trim, seal and flute edges.

4. Bake at 425° until crust is golden brown, 40-45 minutes. Refrigerate leftovers.

1 SLICE: 525 cal., 31g fat (16g sat. fat), 106mg chol., 346mg sod., 49g carb. (23g sugars, 0 fiber), 17g pro.

READER REVIEW
"I love this recipe, and it is my go-to favorite for an easy dessert. Sometimes I tweak it by substituting some cream cheese for a little of the ricotta. Once in a while I substitute raisins for the chocolate chips and add some vanilla and orange extracts, leaving out the orange liqueur. Overall, the texture is wonderful and the results are tasty!"
—DARCYPA, TASTEOFHOME.COM

Peanut Butter Truffle Cupcakes

Everybody loves cupcakes, and these have a wonderfully tasty
hidden treasure tucked inside. They're rich and delicious!
—*Marlene Schollenberger, Bloomington, IN*

PREP: 40 MIN. • **BAKE:** 15 MIN. + COOLING • **MAKES:** 1 DOZEN

6   oz. white baking
    chocolate,
    coarsely chopped
¼   cup creamy
    peanut butter
2   Tbsp. baking cocoa

BATTER
½   cup butter, softened
¾   cup sugar
2   large eggs, room
    temperature
1   tsp. vanilla extract
¾   cup all-purpose flour
½   cup baking cocoa
½   tsp. baking soda
¼   tsp. salt
½   cup buttermilk
½   cup strong brewed
    coffee

FROSTING
3   oz. semisweet
    chocolate, chopped
⅓   cup heavy
    whipping cream
3   Tbsp. creamy
    peanut butter

1. For truffles, in a microwave-safe bowl, melt chocolate at 70% power for 1 minute; stir. Microwave at additional 10- to 20-second intervals, stirring until smooth. Stir in peanut butter. Cover and refrigerate for 15-20 minutes or until firm enough to form into balls. Shape into twelve 1-in. balls; roll in cocoa. Set aside.

2. In a large bowl, cream the butter and sugar until light and fluffy. Add the eggs, 1 at a time, beating well after each addition. Beat in vanilla. Combine the flour, cocoa, baking soda and salt; gradually add to creamed mixture alternately with buttermilk and coffee and mix well.

3. Fill 12 paper-lined muffin cups two-thirds full. Top each with a truffle (do not press down).

4. Bake at 350° until a toothpick inserted in cake portion comes out clean, 15-20 minutes. Cool 10 minutes before removing from pan to a wire rack to cool completely.

5. In a heavy saucepan over low heat, melt chocolate with cream, stirring constantly. Remove from the heat; stir in peanut butter until smooth. Transfer to a small bowl; chill until mixture reaches spreading consistency. Frost cupcakes. Store in the refrigerator.

1 CUPCAKE: 277 cal., 18g fat (8g sat. fat), 66mg chol , 249mg sod., 26g carb. (16g sugars, 2g fiber), 6g pro.

Marble Chiffon Cake

This confection's a real winner—in taste and in looks! It's impressive, but I think that anyone can prepare it, regardless of baking expertise.
—*LuAnn Heikkila, Floodwood, MN*

PREP: 15 MIN. + STANDING • **BAKE:** 1 HOUR + COOLING • **MAKES:** 16 SERVINGS

7 large eggs, separated
2 oz. unsweetened chocolate
1¾ cups sugar, divided
¼ cup hot water
2 cups all-purpose flour
2 tsp. baking powder
1 tsp. salt
¼ tsp. baking soda
¾ cup water
½ cup canola oil
2 tsp. vanilla extract
½ tsp. cream of tartar

FROSTING
4 oz. semisweet chocolate
1 Tbsp. butter
7 Tbsp. heavy whipping cream
1 tsp. vanilla extract
1½ cups confectioners' sugar

1. Let separated eggs stand at room temperature for 30 minutes. In a small saucepan, melt unsweetened chocolate over low heat. Add ¼ cup sugar and hot water; mix well and set aside.

2. In a large bowl, combine the flour, baking powder, salt, baking soda and remaining sugar. Whisk together the egg yolks, water, oil and vanilla; add to the flour mixture and beat until moistened. Beat for 3 minutes on medium speed; set aside.

3. In another large bowl and with clean beaters, beat egg whites and cream of tartar on high speed until stiff peaks form. Fold a fourth of egg whites into the batter, then fold in remaining whites. Divide batter in half; gradually fold chocolate mixture into 1 portion.

4. Alternately spoon the plain and chocolate batters into an ungreased 10-in. tube pan. Swirl with a knife. Bake on the lowest rack at 325° for 60-65 minutes or until top springs back when lightly touched. Immediately invert cake; cool completely. Run a knife around sides and center tube of pan; remove cake to serving plate.

5. For frosting, melt semisweet chocolate and butter in a small saucepan over low heat. Stir in cream and vanilla. Remove from the heat; whisk in confectioners' sugar until smooth. Immediately spoon over cake.

1 SLICE: 363 cal., 17g fat (6g sat. fat), 104mg chol., 256mg sod., 51g carb. (36g sugars, 1g fiber), 5g pro.

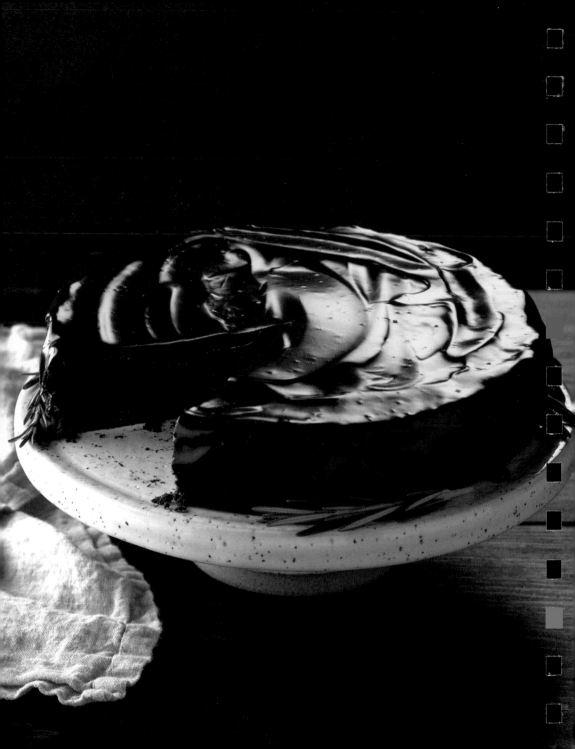

Flourless Chocolate Cake with Rosemary Ganache

This rich cake is the essence of moist, dense and chocolaty.
A silky chocolate ganache infused with rosemary really takes it over the top.
—*Kelly Gardner, Alton, IL*

PREP: 40 MIN. • **BAKE:** 30 MIN. + COOLING • **MAKES:** 16 SERVINGS

1 lb. semisweet chocolate, chopped
1 cup butter, cubed
¼ cup dry red wine
8 large eggs, room temperature
½ cup sugar
1 tsp. vanilla extract

GANACHE
9 oz. bittersweet chocolate, chopped
1 cup heavy whipping cream
2 fresh rosemary sprigs

SWEET SECRET
You can make this cake a day in advance. Cover and refrigerate it, then remove it from the refrigerator 1 hour before serving.

1. Line the bottom of a greased 9-in. springform pan with parchment; grease the paper. Place pan on a double thickness of heavy-duty foil (about 18 in. square). Securely wrap foil around pan; set aside.

2. In a large heavy saucepan, combine the chocolate, butter and wine over low heat, stirring constantly while melting. Remove from the heat. Cool to room temperature.

3. Meanwhile, in a large bowl, beat the eggs, sugar and vanilla until frothy and doubled in volume, about 5 minutes. Gradually fold eggs into chocolate mixture, one-third at a time, until well blended. Pour into the prepared pan. Place springform pan in a large baking pan; add 1 in. of hot water to larger pan.

4. Bake at 350° for 28-32 minutes or until outer edges are set (center will jiggle). Remove springform pan from water bath. Cool completely on a wire rack.

5. Carefully run a knife around edge of pan to loosen; remove sides of pan. Invert onto a serving platter; remove parchment.

6. Place chocolate in a small bowl. In a small saucepan, bring cream and rosemary just to a boil. Remove from the heat; discard the rosemary. Pour cream over chocolate; whisk until smooth. Cool slightly, stirring occasionally. Pour over cake. Chill until set.

1 SLICE: 435 cal., 35g fat (20g sat. fat), 156mg chol., 121mg sod., 31g carb. (26g sugars, 3g fiber), 7g pro.

Chocolate Almond Silk Pie

I've been baking since I was 9 years old. Back then, my friends and I would make chocolate chip cookies. Of all the cooking I do today, I still enjoy baking best.
—*Diane Larson, Roland, IA*

PREP: 20 MIN. + CHILLING • **COOK:** 30 MIN. + COOLING • **MAKES:** 10 SERVINGS

⅔ cup all-purpose flour
¼ cup butter, softened
3 Tbsp. finely chopped almonds, toasted
2 Tbsp. confectioners' sugar
⅛ tsp. vanilla extract

FILLING
¾ cup sugar
3 large eggs
3 oz. unsweetened chocolate, coarsely chopped
⅛ tsp. almond extract
½ cup butter, softened
Sweetened whipped cream and toasted sliced almonds, optional

1. In a small bowl, combine the first 5 ingredients. Beat on low speed until well combined, 2-3 minutes. Press onto the bottom and up the sides of a greased 9-in. pie plate. Bake at 400° for 8-10 minutes or until golden. Cool on a wire rack.

2. For filling, combine sugar and eggs in a small saucepan until well blended. Cook over low heat, stirring constantly until mixture coats the back of a metal spoon and reaches 160°. Remove from the heat. Stir in the chocolate and almond extract until smooth. Cool to lukewarm (90°), stirring occasionally.

3. In a large bowl, cream butter until light and fluffy. Add cooled egg mixture; beat on high speed for 5 minutes. Pour into cooled pie shell. Refrigerate for at least 6 hours before serving. Garnish with whipped cream and almonds if desired. Refrigerate leftovers.

1 SLICE: 293 cal., 21g fat (12g sat. fat), 100mg chol., 120mg sod., 26g carb. (17g sugars, 2g fiber), 5g pro.

SWEET SECRET
You can dress up this heavenly treat with whipped cream and chocolate shavings or curls. In a rush? Garnish with a handful of almonds or even chocolate chips.

Chocolate Pound Cake

This cake goes well with ice cream, but it's also delicate
enough that you can serve small pieces for a tea.
—*Ann Perry, Sierra Vista, AZ*

PREP: 20 MIN. • **BAKE:** 1½ HOURS + COOLING • **MAKES:** 12 SERVINGS

8 **milk chocolate bars
(1.55 oz. each)**
2 **Tbsp. water**
½ **cup butter, softened**
2 **cups sugar**
4 **large eggs, room
temperature**
2 **tsp. vanilla extract**
2½ **cups cake flour, sifted**
½ **tsp. salt**
¼ **tsp. baking soda**
1 **cup buttermilk**
½ **cup chopped pecans,
optional
Confectioners' sugar,
optional**

1. Preheat oven to 325°. In a saucepan, melt chocolate with water over low heat. Mixture will begin to harden.

2. In a large bowl, cream the butter and sugar until light and fluffy. Add the eggs, 1 at a time, beating well after each addition. Beat in vanilla and the chocolate mixture. Combine the flour, salt and soda; add to creamed mixture alternately with buttermilk. Fold in nuts if desired.

3. Pour into a greased and floured 10-in. tube pan or fluted tube pan. Bake for 1½ hours or until a toothpick inserted in the center comes out clean. Let stand for 10 minutes before removing from pan to a wire rack to cool. Sprinkle with confectioners' sugar if desired.

1 SLICE: 353 cal., 11g fat (6g sat. fat), 93mg chol., 248mg sod., 59g carb. (36g sugars, 1g fiber), 5g pro.

READER REVIEW
"This was a very tasty cake! I love chocolate pound cakes and this one did not disappoint. I included the nuts since I'm a big fan of the added taste and texture of nuts. The end result was wonderful!"
—SLVARNER, TASTEOFHOME.COM

Chocolate-Peanut Butter Sheet Cake

I love peanut butter and chocolate, so I combined a few recipes to blend the two flavors into one heavenly sheet cake.
—*Lisa Varner, El Paso, TX*

PREP: 25 MIN. • **BAKE:** 25 MIN. + COOLING • **MAKES:** 15 SERVINGS

2 cups all-purpose flour
2 cups sugar
1 tsp. baking soda
½ tsp. salt
1 cup water
½ cup butter, cubed
½ cup creamy peanut butter
¼ cup baking cocoa
3 large eggs, room temperature
½ cup sour cream
2 tsp. vanilla extract

FROSTING
3 cups confectioners' sugar
½ cup creamy peanut butter
½ cup 2% milk
½ tsp. vanilla extract
½ cup chopped salted or unsalted peanuts

1. Preheat oven to 350°. Grease a 13x9-in. baking pan.

2. In a large bowl, whisk flour, sugar, baking soda and salt. In a small saucepan, combine water, butter, peanut butter and cocoa; bring just to a boil, stirring occasionally. Add to flour mixture, stirring just until moistened.

3. In a small bowl, whisk eggs, sour cream and vanilla until blended; add to flour mixture, whisking constantly. Transfer to prepared pan. Bake until a toothpick inserted in center comes out clean, 25-30 minutes.

4. Prepare frosting while cake is baking. In a large bowl, beat confectioners' sugar, peanut butter, milk and vanilla until smooth.

5. Remove cake from the oven; place on a wire rack. Immediately spread with frosting; sprinkle with peanuts. Cool completely.

1 PIECE: 482 cal., 20g fat (7g sat. fat), 59mg chol., 337mg sod., 70g carb. (53g sugars, 2g fiber), 9g pro.

READER REVIEW
"This is the best cake ever! I made it for my birthday. What a treat! Everyone loved it. This will be a family favorite from now on. I used dark chocolate cocoa. Thank you for sharing this wonderful recipe!"
—USMCMOM8, TASTEOFHOME.COM

Nana's Chocolate Cupcakes with Mint Frosting

Even though she is no longer with us, Nana's treats bring me so much joy every time I bake them. For a more indulgent version, double the frosting and pile it on high!
—*Chekota Hunter, Cassville, MO*

PREP: 25 MIN. • BAKE: 15 MIN. + COOLING • MAKES: 1 DOZEN

½ cup baking cocoa
1 cup boiling water
¼ cup butter, softened
1 cup sugar
2 large eggs, room temperature
1⅓ cups all-purpose flour
2 tsp. baking powder
¼ tsp. salt
¼ cup unsweetened applesauce

FROSTING
1 cup confectioners' sugar
3 Tbsp. butter, softened
4 tsp. heavy whipping cream
    Dash peppermint extract
1 drop green food coloring, optional
2 Tbsp. miniature semisweet chocolate chips
    Mint Andes candies, optional

1. Preheat oven to 375°. Line 12 muffin cups with paper or foil liners. Mix cocoa and boiling water until smooth; cool mixture completely.

2. Beat butter and sugar until blended. Beat in eggs, 1 at a time. In another bowl, whisk together flour, baking powder and salt; add to the butter mixture alternately with the applesauce, beating well after each addition. Beat in the cocoa mixture.

3. Fill prepared muffin cups three-fourths full. Bake until a toothpick inserted in center comes out clean, 15-18 minutes. Cool 10 minutes before removing to a wire rack to cool completely.

4. For frosting, beat confectioners' sugar, butter, cream and extract until smooth. If desired, tint frosting green with food coloring. Stir in chocolate chips. Spread frosting over cupcakes. If desired, top with candies.

1 CUPCAKE: 253 cal., 9g fat (5g sat. fat), 51mg chol., 196mg sod., 41g carb. (28g sugars, 1g fiber), 3g pro.

Contest-Winning German Chocolate Cream Pie

I've won quite a few awards in recipe contests over the years, and I was truly delighted when this luscious pie sent me to the Great American Pie Show finals in Branson, Missouri.
—*Marie Rizzio, Interlochen, MI*

PREP: 20 MIN. • **BAKE:** 45 MIN. + COOLING • **MAKES:** 8 SERVINGS

Pastry for
single-crust pie
4 oz. German sweet
chocolate, chopped
¼ cup butter, cubed
1 can (12 oz.) evaporated
milk
1½ cups sugar
3 Tbsp. cornstarch
Dash salt
2 large eggs
1 tsp. vanilla extract
1⅓ cups sweetened
shredded coconut
½ cup chopped pecans

TOPPING
2 cups heavy
whipping cream
2 Tbsp. confectioners'
sugar
1 tsp. vanilla extract
Additional coconut
and pecans

1. Preheat oven to 375°. On a floured surface, roll dough to fit a 9-in. pie plate. Place in pie plate; trim and flute edge.

2. Place the chocolate and butter in a small saucepan. Cook and stir over low heat until smooth. Remove from the heat; stir in milk. In a large bowl, combine the sugar, cornstarch and salt. Add eggs, vanilla and the chocolate mixture; mix well. Pour into the crust. Sprinkle with coconut and pecans.

3. Bake at 375° until a knife inserted in the center comes out clean, 45-50 minutes. Cool completely on a wire rack.

4. For topping, in a large bowl, beat cream until it begins to thicken. Add confectioners' sugar and vanilla; beat until stiff peaks form. Spread over pie; sprinkle with additional coconut and pecans. Refrigerate until serving.

1 SLICE: 808 cal., 53g fat (30g sat. fat), 168mg chol., 280mg sod., 78g carb. (58g sugars, 3g fiber), 9g pro.

NOTES

CHAPTER 6

Frosty Specialties

Toasted Hazelnut & Chocolate Ice Cream

The flavors in this ice cream take me back to European vacations. I'm a big hazelnut fan who has been caught red-handed eating Nutella out of the jar with a spoon!
—*Laura Majchrzak, Hunt Valley, MD*

PREP: 25 MIN. + CHILLING • **PROCESS:** 15 MIN. + FREEZING • **MAKES:** 8 SERVINGS

- 2 **large eggs**
- ½ **cup sugar**
- ½ **tsp. salt**
- 1 **cup whole milk**
- 1½ **cups heavy whipping cream**
- ½ **cup Nutella**
- 3 **oz. semisweet chocolate, chopped**
- ½ **cup chopped blanched hazelnuts, toasted**

1. In a small heavy saucepan, whisk eggs, sugar and salt until blended; stir in milk. Cook over medium-low heat until a thermometer reads at least 160°, stirring constantly. Do not allow to boil. Remove from heat.

2. Strain into a bowl; whisk in cream and Nutella until smooth. Stir in chopped chocolate. Press plastic wrap onto surface of custard. Refrigerate overnight.

3. Pour custard into cylinder of ice cream freezer; freeze according to manufacturer's directions, adding hazelnuts during the last 2 minutes of processing. Transfer ice cream to freezer containers, allowing headspace for expansion; freeze until firm, 2-4 hours.

½ CUP: 436 cal., 32g fat (15g sat. fat), 101mg chol., 198mg sod., 30g carb. (28g sugars, 2g fiber), 7g pro.

SWEET SECRET
For a special treat, spread a chocolate chip cookie with Nutella. Top with a bit of this ice cream, and sandwich it all with another cookie. Wrap; store in a container in the freezer.

Icebox Cookie Cheesecake

Cookie lovers will come back for seconds when you serve this tempting chocolate treat.
I love that the cheesecake can be made ahead and stored in the freezer.
—*Perlene Hoekema, Lynden, WA*

PREP: 30 MIN. + CHILLING • **MAKES:** 16 SERVINGS

1¼ cups chocolate wafer
    crumbs
  4 **Tbsp. butter, melted**
  2 **cups heavy whipping**
    cream, divided
  3 **pkg. (8 oz. each) cream**
    cheese, softened
  1 **cup sugar**
  1 **pkg. (14.3 oz.) Oreo**
    cookies, quartered
  4 **oz. semisweet**
    chocolate, chopped
  ½ **tsp. vanilla extract**
    Optional:
    Whipped cream and
    chopped Oreo cookies

1. Combine crumbs and butter; press into bottom of a 9- or 10-in. springform pan. Freeze. Whip 1½ cups whipping cream until stiff peaks form; refrigerate.

2. In a large bowl, beat cream cheese until smooth. Gradually add sugar; blend thoroughly. Fold cut cookies into filling along with chilled whipped cream. Spread filling evenly into crust, smoothing top and spreading to edges. Cover and refrigerate 4 hours or overnight. Freeze 1 hour before serving.

3. Meanwhile, melt chocolate in a saucepan over low heat, stirring constantly. Remove from heat; cool slightly. Whisk in vanilla and remaining ½ cup whipping cream. Loosen cheesecake from pan by running knife around edge; remove from pan.

4. Spread chocolate glaze over cheesecake. If desired, top with whipped cream and additional Oreo cookies to serve.

1 PIECE: 523 cal., 37g fat (21g sat. fat), 85mg chol., 320mg sod., 42g carb. (30g sugars, 1g fiber), 5g pro.

NOTES

_____
_____
_____
_____
_____
_____
_____
_____
_____
_____

Dark Chocolate Ice Cream with Paprika & Agave

Pair this rich and creamy ice cream with a cup of hot or iced coffee. The change-of-pace treat is mildly sweet with a hint of paprika.
—Taste of Home *Test Kitchen*

PREP: 30 MIN. + CHILLING • **PROCESS:** 20 MIN./BATCH + FREEZING • **MAKES:** 1 QT.

1 cup whole milk
½ cup agave nectar
2 large eggs
1 tsp. Hungarian paprika
  Dash salt
8 oz. bittersweet chocolate, melted and cooled
2 cups heavy whipping cream
1½ tsp. vanilla extract

1. In a small heavy saucepan, heat milk and agave nectar until bubbles form around sides of pan. In a small bowl, whisk the eggs, paprika and salt. Stir in chocolate. Whisk in a small amount of hot milk mixture. Return all to the pan, whisking constantly.

2. Cook and stir over low heat until mixture is thickened and coats the back of a spoon. Quickly transfer to a bowl; place in ice water and stir for 2 minutes. Stir in cream and vanilla. Press waxed paper onto surface of custard. Refrigerate several hours or overnight.

3. Fill cylinder of ice cream freezer two-thirds full; freeze according to the manufacturer's directions. When ice cream is frozen, transfer to a freezer container; freeze for 2-4 hours before serving.

½ CUP: 446 cal., 36g fat (21g sat. fat), 137mg chol., 71mg sod., 34g carb. (28g sugars, 2g fiber), 6g pro.

Chocolate Peanut Butter Shakes

These rich shakes will make you feel as if you're sitting in a 1950s soda fountain.
—Taste of Home *Test Kitchen*

TAKES: 10 MIN. • MAKES: 2 SERVINGS

¾ cup 2% milk
1½ cups chocolate
    ice cream
¼ cup creamy
    peanut butter
2 Tbsp. chocolate syrup
    Optional toppings:
    Sweetened
    whipped cream,
    miniature peanut butter
    cups, quartered,
    and additional
    chocolate syrup

In a blender, combine the milk, ice cream, peanut butter and syrup; cover and process until smooth. If desired, garnish with whipped cream, peanut butter cups and additional chocolate syrup.

1 CUP: 501 cal., 29g fat (11g sat. fat), 41mg chol., 262mg sod., 51g carb. (43g sugars, 3g fiber), 14g pro.

Macaroon Ice Cream Torte

With four types of chocolate, this frosty dessert is as tasty as it is impressive. You must try it!
—*Barbara Carlucci, Orange Park, FL*

PREP: 20 MIN. + FREEZING • MAKES: 16 SERVINGS

30 chocolate or plain
    macaroon cookies,
    crumbled
1 qt. coffee ice cream,
    softened if necessary
1 qt. chocolate ice
    cream, softened
    if necessary
1 cup milk chocolate
    toffee bits or 4 Heath
    candy bars (1.4 oz.
    each), coarsely
    chopped
    Hot fudge topping

1. Sprinkle a third of the cookies into an ungreased 9-in. springform pan. Layer with 2 cups coffee ice cream, another third of the cookies, 2 cups chocolate ice cream and ½ cup toffee bits; repeat layers.

2. Freeze, covered, until firm. May be frozen for up to 2 months. Remove torte from freezer 10 minutes before slicing. Serve with warmed fudge topping.

1 SLICE: 341 cal., 20g fat (11g sat. fat), 36mg chol., 110mg sod., 37g carb. (35g sugars, 2g fiber), 4g pro.

Chocolate Caramel Hazelnut Pie

I love chocolate, caramel and hazelnuts, so I created a recipe with them all. Place the crust ingredients in a storage bag and smash with a rolling pin if you don't have a food processor.
—*Debbie Anderson, Mount Angel, OR*

PREP: 25 MIN. + CHILLING • **MAKES:** 8 SERVINGS

1½ cups salted caramel
    pretzel pieces
12 Lorna Doone
    shortbread cookies
¼   cup sugar
6   Tbsp. butter, melted
5   Tbsp. caramel topping,
    divided

FILLING
1   pkg. (8 oz.) cream
    cheese, softened
½   cup Nutella
1   jar (7 oz.) marshmallow
    creme
1   carton (8 oz.) frozen
    whipped topping,
    thawed
1   cup miniature
    marshmallows
1   Snickers candy bar
    (1.86 oz.), chopped

1. Place pretzel pieces and cookies in a food processor; pulse until fine crumbs form. Add sugar and melted butter; pulse just until blended. Press onto bottom and sides of a 9-in. pie plate. Drizzle with 3 Tbsp. caramel topping. Freeze while preparing filling.

2. For filling, beat cream cheese and Nutella until smooth. Gradually beat in marshmallow creme. Gently fold in whipped topping and marshmallows. Spoon into crust.

3. Refrigerate until set, 3-4 hours. Top with chopped candy and the remaining 2 Tbsp. caramel topping before serving.

1 SLICE: 663 cal., 35g fat (19g sat. fat), 60mg chol., 327mg sod., 74g carb. (57g sugars, 1g fiber), 6g pro.

SWEET SECRET
If you're short on time, you can quick-chill this pie in the freezer—it will take about 1 hour.

Dark Chocolate Pudding

Life is too short to pass on dessert. This old-fashioned treat is so creamy and comforting!
—*Lily Julow, Lawrenceville, GA*

PREP: 5 MIN. + CHILLING • **COOK:** 20 MIN. + COOLING • **MAKES:** 6 SERVINGS

¼ cup sugar
3 Tbsp. cornstarch
¼ tsp. salt
2 cups whole milk
3 large egg yolks
1 dark chocolate candy bar (6.8 oz.), chopped
½ tsp. vanilla extract
Whipped cream, optional

1. In a large saucepan, mix sugar, cornstarch and salt. Whisk in milk until smooth. Cook and stir over medium heat until thickened and bubbly. Reduce heat to low; cook and stir 2 minutes longer. Remove from heat.

2. In a small bowl, whisk a small amount of hot mixture into egg yolks; return all to pan, whisking constantly. Bring to a gentle boil; cook and stir 2 minutes. Reduce heat to low; stir in chocolate until melted. Remove from heat; stir in vanilla. Cool 15 minutes, stirring occasionally.

3. Transfer to a bowl; press plastic wrap onto surface of pudding. Refrigerate until cold. If desired, serve with whipped cream.

1 SERVING: 266 cal., 15g fat (9g sat. fat), 104mg chol., 138mg sod., 35g carb. (29g sugars, 3g fiber), 6g pro.

SWEET SECRET
Plastic is placed directly on the surface of the pudding to prevent a skin from forming. The skin is actually milk protein (casein) that has dried out because of evaporation. You also can prevent a skin from forming by adding a thin layer of butter: Hold a stick of butter at 1 end and touch the other end to the hot pudding in several places until the butter has melted into a thin layer atop the pudding.

Classic Treat Made Easy

Pudding like Grandma used to make is creamy and delicious. For guaranteed success, see the steps pictured above and follow the recipe at left.

- You can customize the flavors by using almond, orange or mint extracts instead of the vanilla.

- For mocha flavor, stir in 2 tsp. instant espresso powder along with the sugar mixture at the beginning of the recipe.

- Whipped cream is always a welcome garnish, but you can mix things up by topping bowls of pudding with berries, granola or chocolate curls.

Double-Chocolate Toffee Icebox Cake

My mother-in-law taught me that anything tastes good if you use enough chocolate or cream. This no-bake dessert proves she was right.

—Bee Engelhart, Bloomfield Township, MI

PREP: 30 MIN. + CHILLING • MAKES: 8 SERVINGS

3 cups 2% milk
1 pkg. (5.9 oz.) instant chocolate pudding mix
1½ cups heavy whipping cream
2 pkg. (9 oz. each) chocolate wafers
2 Heath candy bars (1.4 oz. each), crushed

1. In a large bowl, whisk milk and pudding mix 2 minutes. Let stand 2 minutes or until soft-set. In another large bowl, beat cream until stiff peaks form.

2. Arrange 20 cookies on bottom of an 8-in. square baking dish. Spread a fourth of the chocolate pudding and a fourth of the whipped cream over cookies. Repeat layers 3 times. Sprinkle with crushed candy bars. Refrigerate overnight.

1 PIECE: 538 cal., 28g fat (14g sat. fat), 64mg chol., 493mg sod., 68g carb. (40g sugars, 3g fiber), 8g pro.

READER REVIEW

"This is one of those recipes that look so much more complicated than they are. When I served it, the whole table went silent as all my friends gobbled it down. Sometimes I vary ingredients— graham wafers instead of chocolate, or a different flavor of pudding. It all turns out great."

—HEXA, TASTEOFHOME.COM

Black Forest Icebox Cookies

Rich chocolate wafers are the perfect complement to the creamy filling's sweet-tart tones. Chill for up to four hours; any longer and the wafers get too soft to pick up with your hands.
—Taste of Home *Test Kitchen*

PREP: 15 MIN. + CHILLING • **COOK:** 5 MIN. + COOLING • **MAKES:** 20 COOKIES

3 Tbsp. sugar
4 tsp. cornstarch
  Dash salt
¾ cup fresh or frozen pitted tart cherries (thawed), coarsely chopped
¾ cup cherry juice blend
1½ tsp. lemon juice
1 to 2 drops red food coloring, optional
½ cup mascarpone cheese
1 Tbsp. confectioners' sugar
1 tsp. cherry brandy
1 pkg. (9 oz.) chocolate wafers
½ cup semisweet chocolate chips
¼ cup heavy whipping cream

1. In a small saucepan, combine the sugar, cornstarch and salt. Add the cherries, juice blend and lemon juice. Bring to a boil; cook and stir until thickened, about 2 minutes. Remove from the heat; stir in food coloring if desired. Cool to room temperature.

2. In a small bowl, combine the mascarpone cheese, confectioners' sugar and brandy. Spread about 1 tsp. cheese mixture onto each of 20 wafers; layer each with 2 tsp. cherry mixture. Top with remaining wafers. Place on a waxed paper-lined baking pan.

3. Place chocolate chips in a small bowl. In a small saucepan, bring cream just to a boil. Pour over chips; whisk until smooth. Drizzle over cookies. Refrigerate, covered, for up to 4 hours before serving.

1 SANDWICH COOKIE: 139 cal., 9g fat (4g sat. fat), 17mg chol., 81mg sod., 15g carb. (9g sugars, 1g fiber), 2g pro.

Creamy Mocha Frozen Dessert

Light as a feather, this cool, satisfying dessert is delicious and impressive to serve.
It's an excellent dessert to make ahead as it can be stored in the freezer.
—*Launa Shoemaker, Landrum, SC*

PREP: 20 MIN. + FREEZING • MAKES: 24 SERVINGS

2 tsp. instant coffee
  granules
1 Tbsp. hot water
1 cup cream-filled
  chocolate cookie
  crumbs
¾ cup chopped pecans,
  divided
¼ cup butter, melted
2 pkg. (8 oz. each) cream
  cheese, softened
1 can (14 oz.) sweetened
  condensed milk
½ cup chocolate syrup
1 carton (8 oz.) frozen
  whipped topping,
  thawed

1. In a small bowl, dissolve coffee granules in hot water; set aside. In another bowl, combine cookie crumbs, ½ cup pecans and butter. Pat into a 13x9-in. dish.

2. In a large bowl, beat cream cheese until light and fluffy. Blend in coffee mixture, milk and chocolate syrup. Fold in whipped topping and spread over crust. Sprinkle the remaining ¼ cup pecans on top. Cover and freeze 4 hours or until firm.

1 PIECE: 202 cal., 12g fat (6g sat. fat), 21mg chol., 103mg sod., 20g carb. (16g sugars, 1g fiber), 3g pro.

SWEET SECRET
Want to mix things up a bit? Beat a tablespoon of peanut butter into the cream cheese mixture.

Mint-Chocolate Ice Cream Cake

This versatile ice cream cake is pretty enough for company and simple enough for a weeknight treat. Try food coloring to tint the whipped topping, or use different flavors of ice cream, extracts, and cookie or candy crumbs to suit different holidays or occasions!
—*Kathy Morrow, Hubbard, OH*

PREP: 15 MIN. + FREEZING • **MAKES:** 10 SERVINGS

2 **pkg. (10 oz. each) individual cream-filled chocolate cakes**
3 **cups mint chocolate chip ice cream, softened**
12 **Oreo cookies, crushed, divided**
2 **cups whipped topping**
½ **tsp. mint extract, optional**

1. Line a 9x5-in. loaf pan with plastic wrap. Place 6 cakes in pan, completely covering the bottom. Spread ice cream over the cakes; sprinkle with half the cookie crumbs. Press remaining cakes on top. Cover and freeze for at least 3 hours.

2. Just before serving, remove from the freezer and invert onto a serving plate. Remove pan and plastic wrap.

3. If desired, combine whipped topping and extract; frost top and sides of cake with whipped topping. Sprinkle with remaining cookie crumbs.

1 SLICE: 382 cal., 18g fat (10g sat. fat), 27mg chol., 340mg sod., 50g carb. (38g sugars, 1g fiber), 4g pro.

Frozen Brownie Bombe

I love making ice cream bombes. They look so elegant yet are incredibly simple to make. This one beautifully pairs chocolate with hazelnuts.
—*Melissa Millwood, Lyman, SC*

PREP: 45 MIN. • **BAKE:** 55 MIN. + FREEZING • **MAKES:** 16 SERVINGS

2 cups semisweet chocolate chips
½ cup butter, cubed
3 large eggs, room temperature
1½ cups sugar
½ tsp. salt
1 tsp. vanilla extract
¾ cup all-purpose flour
3 cups whole hazelnuts, toasted and chopped, divided
3 qt. chocolate ice cream, softened if necessary
½ cup Nutella

1. Preheat oven to 350°. Line bottom of a greased 9-in. springform pan with parchment; grease paper.

2. In a microwave, melt chocolate chips and butter; stir until smooth. Cool slightly. In a large bowl, beat eggs, sugar and salt. Stir in vanilla and the chocolate mixture. Add flour, mixing well. Stir in 1 cup hazelnuts.

3. Spread into prepared pan. Bake 55-60 minutes or until a toothpick inserted in center comes out with moist crumbs (do not overbake). Cool completely in pan on a wire rack.

4. Meanwhile, use plastic wrap to line a 4-qt. bowl with a 9-in.-diameter top. Quickly spread ice cream into bowl. Freeze, covered, until firm.

5. Loosen sides of brownie with a knife; remove rim from pan. Transfer brownie to a serving plate and remove paper. Spread top with Nutella. Invert ice cream mold onto brownie; remove bowl and plastic wrap. Immediately press remaining hazelnuts onto ice cream. Freeze, covered, at least 1 hour before serving. Cut into wedges.

1 SLICE: 960 cal., 62g fat (22g sat. fat), 118mg chol., 278mg sod., 101g carb. (84g sugars, 9g fiber), 15g pro.

Mocha-Pecan Ice Cream Bonbons

These bite-sized bonbons may seem tricky, but you'll find they're a breeze. Keep the recipe handy—as soon as folks sample the treats, they'll ask how to make them!
—Taste of Home *Test Kitchen*

PREP: 25 MIN. + FREEZING • **MAKES:** ABOUT 5 DOZEN

2 **cups finely chopped toasted pecans**
1 **qt. vanilla ice cream or flavor of your choice**
2 **cups semisweet chocolate chips**
½ **cup butter, cubed**
1 **Tbsp. instant coffee granules**

READER REVIEW

"This is my favorite treat to eat during a movie, so now I'm able to make them at home while watching Netflix. You owe it to yourself to try this recipe."

—SALLYGIRL7, TASTEOFHOME.COM

1. Line a 15x10x1-in. baking pan with waxed paper; place in freezer to keep cold. Place pecans in a shallow bowl.

2. Working quickly, scoop ice cream with a melon baller to make ¾-in. balls; immediately roll in pecans. Place on prepared pan; freeze at least 1 hour or until firm.

3. In a microwave, melt the chocolate chips and butter; stir until smooth. Stir in coffee granules until dissolved; cool completely.

4. Working quickly and in batches, use a toothpick to dip ice cream balls into chocolate mixture; allow excess to drip off. Place on a waxed paper-lined pan; remove toothpick. Return to freezer; freeze until set. For longer storage, transfer bonbons to a covered freezer container and return to freezer.

1 BONBON: 171 cal., 14g fat (6g sat. fat), 16mg chol., 46mg sod., 12g carb. (10g sugars, 1g fiber), 2g pro.

Hot Chocolate Tiramisu

Instead of using coffee and rum, I let cinnamon shine in this tiramisu.
It's best if eaten within a few days—if it even lasts that long!
—*Cathy Geniti, Saratoga Springs, NY*

PREP: 25 MIN. • **COOK:** 10 MIN. + CHILLING • **MAKES:** 12 SERVINGS

3 **Tbsp. baking cocoa**
3 **Tbsp. sugar**
2 **Tbsp. water**
2 **cups whole milk**

TIRAMISU
3 **large egg yolks**
1 **cup sugar, divided**
2 **cups mascarpone cheese**
1 **cup heavy whipping cream**
45 **crisp ladyfinger cookies (about 13 oz.)**
¼ **cup miniature semisweet chocolate chips**
2 **tsp. ground cinnamon**

1. For hot cocoa, in a small saucepan, mix cocoa, sugar and water until smooth. Bring to a boil; cook, stirring constantly, 2 minutes. Stir in milk until blended; transfer to a shallow bowl. Cool completely.

2. For tiramisu, in a heatproof bowl of a stand mixer, whisk egg yolks and ½ cup sugar until blended. Place over simmering water in a large saucepan over medium heat. Whisking constantly, heat mixture until a thermometer reads 160°, 2-3 minutes.

3. Remove from heat. With the whisk attachment of a stand mixer, beat on high speed until thick and pale yellow, about 5 minutes. Add mascarpone; beat on medium speed until smooth, scraping down sides of bowl as needed.

4. In another bowl, beat cream until it begins to thicken. Add remaining sugar; beat until soft peaks form. Fold whipped cream into mascarpone mixture.

5. To assemble, spread a third of the cream mixture into a 13x9-in. baking dish. Quickly dip half of the ladyfingers halfway into cooled cocoa; arrange over cream. Repeat layers. Spread with remaining cream mixture. Sprinkle with chocolate chips and cinnamon. Refrigerate, covered, at least 8 hours or overnight.

1 PIECE: 638 cal., 46g fat (25g sat. fat), 199mg chol., 112mg sod., 49g carb. (38g sugars, 1g fiber), 11g pro.

Cherry Chocolate Ice Cream Pie

You may want to make two of these easy ice cream pies—one to serve and the other to store in the freezer for company. The combination of chocolate and cherries is irresistible.

—*Lisa Varner, El Paso, TX*

PREP: 15 MIN. + FREEZING • **MAKES:** 8 SERVINGS

¾ cup dried cherries
2 cups boiling water
3½ cups chocolate ice cream, softened
¾ cup miniature semisweet chocolate chips
1 chocolate crumb crust (9 in.)
   Optional: Hot fudge ice cream topping and maraschino cherries

1. Place dried cherries in a small bowl; cover with boiling water. Let stand for 5 minutes; drain.

2. In a large bowl, combine the ice cream, chocolate chips and cherries. Spread into crust. Cover the pie and freeze until firm.

3. Slice. If desired, drizzle each piece with fudge topping and garnish with a maraschino cherry.

1 SLICE: 344 cal., 16g fat (8g sat. fat), 20mg chol., 148mg sod., 50g carb. (39g sugars, 3g fiber), 5g pro.

NOTES

Frozen Mocha Marbled Loaf

A creamy blend of chocolate, coffee and cheesecake make up the frosty slices in this beautiful marbled treat. I know it's perfect for summer, but I make it all year.
—*Cheryl Martinetto, Grand Rapids, MN*

PREP: 15 MIN. + FREEZING • **MAKES:** 12 SERVINGS

- 2 **cups finely crushed Oreo cookies (about 20 cookies)**
- 3 **Tbsp. butter, melted**
- 1 **pkg. (8 oz.) cream cheese, softened**
- 1 **can (14 oz.) sweetened condensed milk**
- 1 **tsp. vanilla extract**
- 2 **cups heavy whipping cream, whipped**
- 2 **Tbsp. instant coffee granules**
- 1 **Tbsp. hot water**
- ½ **cup chocolate syrup**

1. Line a 9x5-in. loaf pan with foil. In a bowl, combine the cookie crumbs and butter. Press firmly onto the bottom and 1½ in. up the sides of prepared pan.

2. In a large bowl, beat cream cheese until light and fluffy. Add milk and vanilla and mix well. Fold in whipped cream. Spoon half of the mixture into another bowl and set aside. Dissolve coffee in hot water; fold into remaining cream cheese mixture. Fold in chocolate syrup.

3. Spoon half of the chocolate mixture over crust. Top with half of the reserved cream cheese mixture. Repeat layers. Cut through layers with a knife to swirl the chocolate (pan will be full). Cover and freeze for 6 hours or overnight.

4. To serve, lift out of the pan; remove foil. Cut into slices.

1 SLICE: 490 cal., 32g fat (18g sat. fat), 94mg chol., 275mg sod., 45g carb. (36g sugars, 2g fiber), 7g pro.

Smooth Chocolate Pie

My mom and I created this unbelievable chocolate pie, and our whole family really enjoyed it. We think you will, too.
—*Steve Riemersma, Allegan, MI*

PREP: 25 MIN. + FREEZING • MAKES: 8 SERVINGS

1½ cups finely crushed chocolate wafers (about 24 wafers)
⅓ cup butter, melted
3 oz. cream cheese, softened
2 Tbsp. sugar
4 oz. German sweet chocolate, melted
⅓ cup 2% milk
1 carton (8 oz.) frozen whipped topping, thawed
Additional melted German sweet chocolate, optional

1. In a small bowl, mix wafer crumbs and melted butter. Press onto bottom and up sides of an ungreased 9-in. pie plate.

2. In a bowl, beat cream cheese and sugar until blended. Gradually beat in melted chocolate and milk. Refrigerate 10 minutes.

3. Fold whipped topping into chocolate mixture; spoon into crust. Freeze 4 hours or until firm. If desired, drizzle with melted chocolate before serving.

1 SLICE: 383 cal., 24g fat (15g sat. fat), 33mg chol., 293mg sod., 39g carb. (23g sugars, 2g fiber), 4g pro.

NOTES

_____
_____
_____
_____
_____
_____

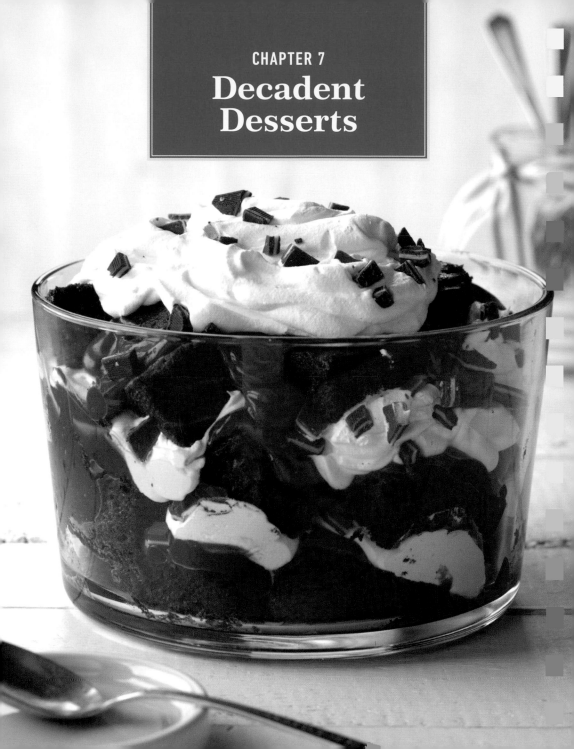

Irish Creme Chocolate Trifle

I had both Irish creme creamer and minty candies on hand, so I created this delicious trifle. It's rich, decadent and easy to put together.
—*Margaret Wilson, San Bernardino, CA*

PREP: 20 MIN. + CHILLING • **BAKE:** 30 MIN. + COOLING • **MAKES:** 16 SERVINGS

1 pkg. devil's food cake mix (regular size)
1 cup refrigerated Irish creme nondairy creamer
3½ cups 2% milk
2 pkg. (3.9 oz. each) instant chocolate pudding mix
3 cups whipped topping
12 mint Andes candies, chopped

READER REVIEW

"My friend always wants me to bring this—Christmas, birthdays, whatever. I use the green striped mints crushed in the layers and on top. They are pretty and add a little crunch."

—MARTHALJ, TASTEOFHOME.COM

1. Prepare and bake cake mix according to package directions, using a 13x9-in. pan. Cool in pan on a wire rack 1 hour.

2. With a meat fork or wooden skewer, poke holes in cake about 2 in. apart. Slowly pour creamer over cake; refrigerate, covered, 1 hour.

3. In a large bowl, whisk milk and the pudding mixes 2 minutes; let stand until soft-set, about 2 minutes.

4. Cut cake into 1½-in. cubes. In a 3-qt. trifle or glass bowl, layer a third of each of the following: cake cubes, pudding, whipped topping and candies. Repeat layers twice. Refrigerate until serving.

1 SERVING: 343 cal., 14g fat (5g sat. fat), 39mg chol., 363mg sod., 49g carb. (32g sugars, 1g fiber), 5g pro.

Chocolate Hazelnut Torte

Most chocolate cake recipes feed a crowd. So we came up with this elegant little cake that serves six. That's enough for two—with just the right amount of leftovers!
—Taste of Home *Test Kitchen*

PREP: 30 MIN. + CHILLING • **BAKE:** 25 MIN. + COOLING • **MAKES:** 6 SERVINGS

⅓ cup butter, softened
1 cup packed
   brown sugar
1 large egg, room
   temperature
1 tsp. vanilla extract
1 cup all-purpose flour
¼ cup baking cocoa
1 tsp. baking soda
⅛ tsp. salt
½ cup sour cream
½ cup brewed coffee,
   room temperature

FROSTING
7 oz. semisweet
   chocolate, chopped
1 cup heavy
   whipping cream
2 Tbsp. sugar
⅓ cup Nutella
   Optional: Chocolate
   curls and hazelnuts

1. In a small bowl, cream butter and brown sugar until light and fluffy, 5-7 minutes. Beat in egg and vanilla. Combine the flour, cocoa, baking soda and salt; gradually add to creamed mixture alternately with sour cream and coffee. Beat just until combined.

2. Pour into 2 greased and floured 6-in. round baking pans. Bake at 350° for 25-30 minutes or until a knife inserted in the center comes out clean. Cool for 10 minutes before removing from pans to wire racks to cool completely.

3. For frosting, in a small saucepan, melt chocolate with cream and sugar over low heat; stir until smooth. Remove from the heat; whisk in Nutella. Transfer to a small bowl; cover and refrigerate until frosting reaches spreading consistency, stirring occasionally.

4. Spread frosting between layers and over top and sides of the cake. If desired, garnish cake with chocolate curls and hazelnuts.

1 SLICE: 768 cal., 45g fat (25g sat. fat), 130mg chol., 386mg sod., 89g carb. (66g sugars, 4g fiber), 9g pro.

Fudge Pecan Brownie Tart

I love inventing my own recipes and entering contests. I'm happy to say that I won a blue ribbon at the Iowa State Fair for this one.
—*Gloria Kratz, Des Moines, IA*

PREP: 30 MIN. • **BAKE:** 30 MIN. • **MAKES:** 12 SERVINGS

1   cup all-purpose flour
¼   cup packed light brown sugar
¼   cup finely chopped pecans
½   cup cold butter
2   Tbsp. 2% milk
1   tsp. vanilla extract

BROWNIE FILLING
3   oz. unsweetened chocolate
½   cup chocolate chips
½   cup butter, cut into pieces
1½ cups sugar
3   large eggs, room temperature
2   tsp. vanilla extract
¾   cup all-purpose flour
1   cup chopped pecans

FUDGE FROSTING
1½ oz. unsweetened chocolate
⅔   cup sweetened condensed milk
¼   cup butter
1   large egg yolk, beaten
½   tsp. vanilla extract
    Optional: Whipped cream and whole pecans

1. Combine flour, brown sugar and nuts in a large bowl; cut in butter until mixture resembles coarse meal. Mix in milk and vanilla with a fork just until blended. Pat onto bottom and up the sides of an 11-in. tart pan; set aside.

2. For filling, melt chocolate and chips in the top of a double boiler over hot water. Remove from heat and stir in butter. Place in a large bowl and combine with sugar. Add eggs and vanilla; blend well. Gradually add flour, blending well after each addition. Add nuts. Pour over crust.

3. Bake at 350° until center is just set and toothpick comes out clean, 30-35 minutes. Cool on wire rack.

4. Meanwhile, for frosting, melt chocolate in a small saucepan over low heat. Add milk, butter, yolk and vanilla. Heat, stirring vigorously, until smooth and thick, about 5 minutes. Spread over tart. Garnish with whipped cream and pecans if desired.

1 SLICE: 580 cal., 37g fat (17g sat. fat), 128mg chol., 236mg sod., 61g carb. (43g sugars, 3g fiber), 7g pro.

SWEET SECRET
Hang on to this frosting recipe. You'll want to use it on your cupcakes, brownies and even cookies! It's an exceptional way to add homemade flair to baked goods that start with a mix.

Mocha Yule Log

This dessert is guaranteed to delight your holiday guests, especially the chocolate lovers!
—*Jenny Hughson, Mitchell, NE*

PREP: 65 MIN. + CHILLING • **BAKE:** 15 MIN. + COOLING • **MAKES:** 12 SERVINGS

5 large eggs, separated
½ cup cake flour
¼ cup baking cocoa
¼ tsp. salt
1 cup sugar, divided
½ tsp. cream of tartar

FILLING
1½ tsp. instant coffee
    granules
1 cup heavy
    whipping cream
½ cup confectioners'
    sugar

FROSTING
⅓ cup butter, softened
2 cups confectioners'
    sugar
⅓ cup baking cocoa
1 Tbsp. brewed coffee,
    cooled
1½ tsp. vanilla extract
2 to 3 Tbsp. 2% milk

1. Place egg whites in a small bowl; let stand at room temperature 30 minutes.

2. Meanwhile, preheat oven to 350°. Line bottom of a greased 15x10x1-in. pan with parchment; grease parchment. Sift flour, cocoa and salt together twice. In a large bowl, beat egg yolks until slightly thickened. Gradually add ½ cup sugar, beating on high speed until thick and lemon-colored. Fold in flour mixture.

3. Add cream of tartar to egg whites; with clean beaters, beat on medium until soft peaks form. Gradually add remaining sugar, 1 Tbsp. at a time, beating on high after each addition until sugar is dissolved. Continue beating until soft glossy peaks form. Fold a fourth of the whites into batter, then fold in remaining whites. Transfer to prepared pan, spreading evenly.

4. Bake until the top springs back when lightly touched, 12-15 minutes (do not overbake). Cool 5 minutes. Invert onto a tea towel dusted lightly with cocoa. Gently peel off parchment. Roll up cake in the towel jelly-roll style, starting with a short side. Cool completely on a wire rack.

5. For filling, in a bowl, dissolve coffee granules in cream; beat until it begins to thicken. Add sugar; beat until stiff peaks form. Unroll cake; spread filling over cake to within ½ in. of edges. Roll up again, without towel; trim ends. Transfer to a platter, seam side down. Refrigerate, covered, until cold.

6. Beat frosting ingredients until smooth. Spread over cake. Make lines in frosting with fork. Refrigerate until serving.

1 SLICE: 341 cal., 15g fat (8g sat. fat), 130mg chol., 136mg sod., 49g carb. (40g sugars, 1g fiber), 4g pro.

How to Make Whipped Cream

Liven up any dessert with a dollop (or two) of this all-time favorite garnish.

- In a chilled glass bowl, beat 1 cup heavy whipping cream until it begins to thicken. It should have some body but not yet form definite peaks.

- Add 3 Tbsp. confectioners' sugar and ½ tsp. vanilla extract. Continue beating until soft peaks form.

Semisweet Chocolate Mousse

A friend shared this rich, velvety mousse recipe with me. I love to cook and have tons of recipes, but this one is a favorite. Best of all, it's easy to make.
—*Judy Spencer, San Diego, CA*

PREP: 20 MIN. + CHILLING • **MAKES:** 2 SERVINGS

¼ cup semisweet
    chocolate chips
1   Tbsp. water
1   large egg yolk,
    lightly beaten
1½ tsp. vanilla extract
½   cup heavy whipping
    cream
1   Tbsp. sugar
    Optional: Whipped
    cream and raspberries

1. In a small saucepan, melt chocolate chips with water; stir until smooth. Stir a small amount of hot chocolate mixture into egg yolk; return all to the pan, stirring constantly. Cook and stir for 2 minutes or until slightly thickened. Remove from the heat; stir in vanilla. Quickly transfer to a small bowl. Stir occasionally until mixture is completely cooled.

2. In a small bowl, beat whipping cream until it begins to thicken. Add sugar; beat until soft peaks form. Fold into cooled chocolate mixture. Cover and refrigerate for at least 2 hours. If desired, garnish with whipped cream and raspberries.

1 CUP: 367 cal., 31g fat (18g sat. fat), 188mg chol., 29mg sod., 21g carb. (20g sugars, 1g fiber), 3g pro.

Chocolate Peanut Butter Cheesecake

Family and friends always ooh and aah when I bring out this tempting cheesecake after special dinners. It's truly a showstopper.
—*H.L. Sosnowski, Grand Island, NY*

PREP: 40 MIN. • **BAKE:** 65 MIN. + CHILLING • **MAKES:** 12 SERVINGS

BROWNIE CRUST
- ¼ cup butter, cubed
- 3 oz. unsweetened chocolate
- 1 cup packed brown sugar
- 2 large eggs, room temperature
- 1½ tsp. vanilla extract
- ⅔ cup all-purpose flour
- ⅛ tsp. baking powder
- 1 oz. semisweet chocolate, chopped

FILLING
- 1 jar (12 oz.) creamy peanut butter
- 11 oz. cream cheese, softened
- 1 cup packed brown sugar
- 3 large eggs, room temperature
- ½ cup sour cream

TOPPING
- ¾ cup sour cream
- 2 tsp. sugar
- Optional: Salted peanuts and melted semisweet chocolate

1. In a microwave, melt butter and unsweetened chocolate; stir until smooth. Set aside. In a large bowl, beat brown sugar and eggs until light and fluffy, about 4 minutes. Beat in chocolate mixture and vanilla. Combine flour and baking powder; gradually add to batter and mix well. Stir in the chopped chocolate.

2. Spread 1 cup into a greased 9-in. springform pan. Cover and refrigerate remaining batter. Place pan on a baking sheet. Bake at 350° for 17-19 minutes or until a toothpick inserted in the center comes out clean. Cool on a wire rack for 5 minutes; place in freezer for 15 minutes.

3. For filling, in a large bowl, beat the peanut butter, cream cheese and brown sugar until smooth. Add eggs and sour cream; beat on low speed just until combined. Spread remaining brownie batter about 1½ in. high around sides of pan, sealing to baked crust.

4. Pour filling into center. Bake at 350° for 45 minutes or until center is almost set.

5. For topping, combine sour cream and sugar; spread over filling to within ¾ in. of edges. Return cheesecake to the oven; turn oven off and let stand for 5 minutes. Cool on a wire rack for 10 minutes. Carefully run a knife around pan to loosen; cool 1 hour longer. Refrigerate overnight. If desired, top with peanuts and drizzle with melted chocolate. Refrigerate leftovers.

1 SLICE: 564 cal., 36g fat (16g sat. fat), 144mg chol., 306mg sod., 51g carb. (41g sugars, 2g fiber), 14g pro.

Chocolate Hazelnut Gateau

Gateau (pronounces ga-toe) is the French word for any rich and fancy cake.
I think you'll agree this dense chocolate dessert fits that description!
—Michelle Krzmarzick, Torrance, CA

PREP: 20 MIN. • **BAKE:** 30 MIN. + COOLING • **MAKES:** 12 SERVINGS

⅔ cup butter, softened
¾ cup sugar
3 large eggs, separated,
   room temperature
1 cup semisweet
   chocolate chips,
   melted and cooled
1 tsp. vanilla extract
¾ cup all-purpose flour
½ tsp. salt
¼ cup 2% milk
⅔ cup ground hazelnuts,
   toasted

GLAZE

3 Tbsp. butter
2 Tbsp. light corn syrup
1 Tbsp. water
1 cup semisweet
   chocolate chips
   Toasted slivered
   almonds and fresh
   mint leaves

1. In a large bowl, cream butter and sugar until light and fluffy, 5-7 minutes. Beat in egg yolks, melted chocolate and vanilla. Combine the flour and salt; gradually add to creamed mixture alternately with milk, beating well after each addition. Stir in the hazelnuts.

2. In a small bowl, beat egg whites until stiff peaks form; carefully fold into batter. Spread into a greased 9-in. springform pan. Place pan on a baking sheet.

3. Bake at 350° for 30-35 minutes or until a toothpick inserted in the center comes out clean. Cool on wire rack for 10 minutes. Carefully run a knife around edge of pan to loosen; remove sides of pan. Cool completely.

4. For glaze, in a saucepan, bring the butter, corn syrup and water to a boil, stirring constantly. Remove from the heat. Add the chocolate chips; stir until smooth. Cool to room temperature. Spread over top and sides of cake. Garnish with almonds and mint.

1 SLICE: 384 cal., 25g fat (14g sat. fat), 89mg chol., 256mg sod., 40g carb. (31g sugars, 2g fiber), 4g pro.

> **SWEET SECRET**
> Swap in black walnuts, pecans or even almonds in place of the hazelnuts.

Chocolate & Raspberry Cheesecake

You'll fall in love with this sweet specialty. Each silky slice is topped with juicy raspberries. It proves that you can enjoy cheesecake without breaking a calorie budget.
—Taste of Home *Test Kitchen*

PREP: 25 MIN. + CHILLING • MAKES: 12 SERVINGS

¾ cup graham cracker crumbs
2 Tbsp. butter, melted
1 envelope unflavored gelatin
1 cup cold water
4 oz. semisweet chocolate, coarsely chopped
4 pkg. (8 oz. each) fat-free cream cheese
Sugar substitute equivalent to 1 cup sugar
½ cup sugar
¼ cup baking cocoa
2 tsp. vanilla extract
2 cups fresh raspberries

1. Combine cracker crumbs and butter; press onto bottom of a greased 9-in. springform pan. Bake at 375° until lightly browned, 8-10 minutes. Cool in pan on a wire rack.

2. For filling, in a small saucepan, sprinkle gelatin over cold water; let stand for 1 minute. Heat over low heat, stirring until gelatin is completely dissolved. Add the semisweet chocolate; stir until melted.

3. In a large bowl, beat the cream cheese, sugar substitute and sugar until smooth. Gradually add chocolate mixture and the cocoa. Beat in vanilla. Pour onto crust; refrigerate for 2-3 hours or until firm.

4. Arrange raspberries on top of cheesecake. Carefully run a knife around edge of pan to loosen.

1 SLICE: 237 cal., 7g fat (4g sat. fat), 14mg chol., 576mg sod., 27g carb. (17g sugars, 2g fiber), 14g pro. **DIABETIC EXCHANGES:** 2 starch, 1 lean meat, 1 fat.

NOTES

Sachertorte

Guests will be surprised to hear that this dessert starts with a convenient cake mix.
Each bite features the heavenly combo of chocolate, almonds and apricots.
—Taste of Home *Test Kitchen*

PREP: 30 MIN. • BAKE: 25 MIN. + CHILLING • MAKES: 16 SERVINGS

½ cup chopped dried
   apricots
½ cup amaretto
1 pkg. devil's food cake
   mix (regular size)
3 large eggs, room
   temperature
¾ cup water
⅓ cup canola oil

FILLING
⅔ cup apricot preserves
1 Tbsp. amaretto

GLAZE
1 cup heavy
   whipping cream
¼ cup light corn syrup
12 oz. semisweet
   chocolate, chopped
4 tsp. vanilla extract
1 cup toasted sliced
   almonds, optional

1. Preheat oven to 350°. Combine apricots and amaretto;
let stand 15 minutes. In another bowl, combine cake mix,
eggs, water, oil and apricot mixture. Beat on low speed
30 seconds; beat on medium 2 minutes.

2. Pour into 2 greased and floured 9-in. round baking pans.
Bake until a toothpick inserted in center comes out clean,
22-27 minutes. Cool in pans 10 minutes before removing
to a wire rack to cool completely.

3. For filling, heat apricot preserves and amaretto on low
in a small saucepan, stirring occasionally, until preserves
are melted; set aside.

4. For glaze, combine cream and corn syrup in a small
saucepan. Bring just to a boil. Pour over chocolate; whisk
until smooth. Stir in vanilla.

5. Using a long serrated knife, cut each cake horizontally
in half. Place 1 layer on a serving plate; spread with half
of the filling. Top with another layer; spread with a third
of the glaze. Cover with third layer and remaining filling.
Top with remaining layer; spread top and sides of torte
with remaining glaze. If desired, spread toasted almonds
on edges or sides of torte. Refrigerate several hours
before slicing.

1 SLICE: 415 cal., 21g fat (9g sat. fat), 52mg chol., 281mg sod.,
44g carb. (30g sugars, 2g fiber), 5g pro.

Chocolate-Raspberry Creme Brulee

Just when I thought nothing could beat creme brulee, I created this decadent version that stars rich chocolate and sweet raspberries.
—*Jan Valdez, Chicago, IL*

PREP: 25 MIN. • BAKE: 40 MIN. + CHILLING • MAKES: 10 SERVINGS

- 8 oz. semisweet chocolate, chopped
- 4 cups heavy whipping cream
- ½ cup plus 2 Tbsp. sugar, divided
- 8 large egg yolks, beaten
- 1 Tbsp. vanilla extract
- 30 fresh raspberries
- 2 Tbsp. brown sugar
  Additional fresh raspberries, optional

READER REVIEW
"This was beyond delicious! With rich, deep and downright beautiful flavors, this is a treat that I cannot wait to make again!"
—CATLOVESBOOKS, TASTEOFHOME.COM

1. Place chocolate in a large bowl. In a large saucepan, bring cream and ½ cup sugar just to a boil. Pour over chocolate; whisk until smooth. Slowly stir hot cream mixture into egg yolks; stir in vanilla.

2. Place 3 raspberries in each of 10 ungreased 6-oz. ramekins or custard cups. Evenly divide custard among ramekins. Place in a baking pan; add 1 in. of boiling water to pan. Bake, uncovered, at 325° for 40-50 minutes or until centers are just set (custard will jiggle). Remove ramekins from water bath; cool 10 minutes. Cover and refrigerate for at least 4 hours.

3. Combine brown sugar and the remaining 2 Tbsp. sugar.

4. If using a creme brulee torch, sprinkle custards with sugar mixture. Heat sugar with the torch until caramelized. Serve immediately.

5. If broiling the custards, place ramekins on a baking sheet; let stand at room temperature for 15 minutes. Sprinkle with sugar mixture. Broil 8 in. from the heat until sugar is caramelized, 4-7 minutes. Refrigerate until firm, 1-2 hours. If desired, top with additional fresh raspberries.

1 SERVING: 549 cal., 46g fat (27g sat. fat), 294mg chol., 44mg sod., 32g carb. (27g sugars, 2g fiber), 6g pro.

Chocolate Malt Cheesecake

For a change of pace, you can substitute pretzel crumbs for the graham cracker crumbs. They make a wonderful crust, too.
—*Anita Moffett, Rewey, WI*

PREP: 25 MIN. • BAKE: 1 HOUR + CHILLING • MAKES: 14 SERVINGS

1 cup graham cracker crumbs (about 16 squares)
¼ cup sugar
⅓ cup butter, melted

FILLING
3 pkg. (8 oz. each) cream cheese, softened
1 can (14 oz.) sweetened condensed milk
¾ cup chocolate malt powder
4 large eggs, room temperature, lightly beaten
1 cup semisweet chocolate chips, melted and cooled
1 tsp. vanilla extract
Optional: Confectioners' sugar and chocolate curls

1. Combine cracker crumbs, sugar and butter. Press onto the bottom of a greased 9-in. springform pan; set aside.

2. In a large bowl, beat cream cheese and milk until smooth. Add malt powder; beat well. Add eggs; beat on low speed just until combined. Stir in melted chocolate and vanilla just until blended. Pour over crust. Place pan on a baking sheet.

3. Bake at 325° until center is almost set, 60-65 minutes. Cool on a wire rack for 10 minutes. Carefully run a knife around edge of pan to loosen; cool 1 hour longer. Refrigerate overnight, covering when completely cooled.

4. Remove sides of pan. Garnish with confectioners' sugar and chocolate curls if desired. Refrigerate leftovers.

1 SLICE: 369 cal., 19g fat (11g sat. fat), 101mg chol., 291mg sod., 47g carb. (35g sugars, 1g fiber), 7g pro.

READER REVIEW
"So delicious! I baked this for Easter. It was the first time I've ever tried to make cheesecake. It turned out beautifully—no cracking or bubbling. The cheesecake received rave reviews from the whole gang, and I was asked by four people for the recipe. This treat made me look like a top chef!"
—MARYHODGES, TASTEOFHOME.COM

Neapolitan Cheesecake

This rich, creamy cheesecake has two wonderful chocolate layers:
semisweet and white. An additional strawberry layer really puts it over the top.
—*Sherri Regalbuto, Carp, ON*

PREP: 35 MIN. • **BAKE:** 70 MIN. + CHILLING • **MAKES:** 14 SERVINGS

1 cup chocolate wafer
crumbs (18 wafers)
3 Tbsp. butter, melted

FILLING
3 pkg. (8 oz. each) cream
cheese, softened
¾ cup sugar
¼ cup heavy
whipping cream
3 large eggs,
room temperature,
lightly beaten
1 tsp. vanilla extract
2 oz. semisweet
chocolate, melted
and cooled
2 oz. white baking
chocolate, melted
and cooled
⅓ cup mashed frozen
sweetened sliced
strawberries,
well-drained
Red liquid food
coloring, optional

TOPPING
3 oz. semisweet
chocolate, chopped
2 Tbsp. butter
2 tsp. shortening, divided
1 oz. white baking
chocolate

1. In a small bowl, combine wafer crumbs and butter.
Press onto the bottom of an ungreased 9-in. springform
pan. Place pan on a baking sheet. Bake at 350° for
10 minutes. Cool on a wire rack. Reduce heat to 325°.

2. In a large bowl, beat cream cheese until smooth.
Gradually beat in sugar and cream. Add eggs and vanilla;
beat on low just until combined. Divide batter into thirds.
Add melted semisweet chocolate to a third. Spread over
crust. Add melted white chocolate to another third. Spread
over semisweet layer. Stir strawberries and, if desired, a
few drops of food coloring into remaining portion. Spread
over white chocolate layer. Place the pan on a double
thickness of heavy-duty foil (about 18 in. square). Securely
wrap foil around pan.

3. Place springform pan in a large baking pan. Fill larger
pan with hot water to a depth of 1 in. Bake at 325° for
70-75 minutes or until center is just set. Remove the
springform pan from water bath. Cool on a wire rack for
10 minutes. Remove foil. Carefully run a knife around the
edge of pan to loosen; cool for 1 hour longer. Refrigerate
overnight.

4. For topping, melt semisweet chocolate, butter and 1 tsp.
shortening in a heavy saucepan or microwave; stir until
smooth. Cool 5 minutes. Remove sides of pan. Pour melted
chocolate mixture over cheesecake. Melt white chocolate
and remaining shortening. Drizzle over the cheesecake.
Refrigerate until chocolate is firm. Refrigerate leftovers.

1 SLICE: 265 cal., 18g fat (10g sat. fat), 82mg chol., 157mg
sod., 25g carb. (18g sugars, 1g fiber), 4g pro.

Black Forest Chocolate Torte

This cherry-crowned beauty stacked with layers of chocolate cake and cream filling will have everyone talking.
—*Doris Grotz, York, NE*

PREP: 1 HOUR • **BAKE:** 15 MIN. + COOLING • **MAKES:** 16 SERVINGS

⅔ cup butter, softened
1¾ cups sugar
4 large eggs, room temperature
1¼ cups water
4 oz. unsweetened chocolate, chopped
1 tsp. vanilla extract
1¾ cups all-purpose flour
1 tsp. baking powder
¼ tsp. baking soda

CHOCOLATE FILLING
6 oz. German sweet chocolate, chopped
¾ cup butter, cubed
½ cup sliced almonds, toasted

WHIPPED CREAM
2 cups heavy whipping cream
1 Tbsp. sugar
1½ tsp. vanilla extract

TOPPING
1½ cups sliced almonds, toasted
1 cup cherry pie filling

1. Preheat oven to 350°. Line bottoms of 4 greased 9-in. round baking pans with parchment; grease parchment.

2. Cream the butter and sugar until light and fluffy, 5-7 minutes. Add eggs, 1 at a time, beating well after each addition. Beat in water just until blended.

3. In a microwave, melt unsweetened chocolate; stir until smooth. Stir in vanilla. In a small bowl, whisk together flour, baking powder and baking soda; add to creamed mixture alternately with chocolate mixture, beating after each addition. Divide batter among prepared pans.

4. Bake until a toothpick inserted in center comes out clean, 15-20 minutes. Cool 10 minutes before removing from pans to wire racks; remove paper. Cool completely.

5. For chocolate filling, melt chocolate in a microwave; stir until smooth. Stir in butter until blended. Stir in almonds.

6. For whipped cream, in a small bowl, beat cream until it begins to thicken. Add sugar and vanilla; beat until soft peaks form.

7. To assemble, place 1 cake layer on a serving plate; spread with ⅓ cup chocolate filling and 1 cup whipped cream. Repeat layers twice. Top with the remaining cake and chocolate filling.

8. Spread remaining whipped cream over sides of cake. Press almonds onto sides. Spoon pie filling over top of cake. Refrigerate until serving.

1 SLICE: 596 cal., 41g fat (22g sat. fat), 124mg chol., 210mg sod., 46g carb. (26g sugars, 3g fiber), 8g pro.

Dark Chocolate Truffle Tart

Espresso enhances and intensifies the dark chocolate flavor of my tart. I make the crust with toasted walnuts and dust the cooled dessert with baking cocoa before serving.
—*Johnna Johnson, Scottsdale, AZ*

PREP: 20 MIN. + CHILLING • **BAKE:** 20 MIN. + COOLING • **MAKES:** 12 SERVINGS

⅓ cup confectioners' sugar

⅓ cup walnut halves, toasted

½ cup all-purpose flour

3 Tbsp. baking cocoa

⅛ tsp. salt

⅓ cup cold unsalted butter, cubed

FILLING

8 oz. semisweet chocolate, chopped

¼ cup unsalted butter

⅔ cup heavy whipping cream

1¼ tsp. instant espresso powder

2 large eggs, room temperature, lightly beaten

1 large egg yolk, room temperature

⅓ cup sugar

1½ tsp. vanilla extract

Additional baking cocoa

1. Preheat oven to 350°. Place confectioners' sugar and walnuts in a food processor; pulse until walnuts are finely chopped. Add flour, cocoa and salt; pulse until blended. Add butter; pulse until mixture resembles coarse crumbs.

2. Press dough onto bottom and up sides of a greased 9-in. fluted tart pan with removable bottom. Refrigerate 30 minutes. Bake 10 minutes.

3. Meanwhile, for filling, in a double boiler or metal bowl over hot water, melt chocolate and butter; stir until smooth. Stir in cream and espresso powder. Remove from heat; cool slightly. Whisk in eggs, egg yolk, sugar and vanilla.

4. Pour filling into warm crust. Bake 20-25 minutes or until center is just set (mixture will jiggle). Cool completely on a wire rack. Dust with cocoa before serving.

1 SLICE: 326 cal., 24g fat (13g sat. fat), 85mg chol., 42mg sod., 19g carb. (13g sugars, 1g fiber), 4g protein.

NOTES

_____

_____

_____

_____

_____

_____

_____

_____

Ganache-Topped Chocolate Delight

To say this cake is elegant would be an understatement. It's worthy of special occasions, but it's so easy to whip together that you can enjoy it any day of the week.
—Taste of Home *Test Kitchen*

PREP: 20 MIN. • **BAKE:** 20 MIN. + COOLING • **MAKES:** 12 SERVINGS

¾ cup boiling water
2 oz. 53% cacao dark baking chocolate, coarsely chopped
2 Tbsp. butter
¾ cup sugar
¼ cup buttermilk
1 large egg, room temperature
1 tsp. vanilla extract
½ tsp. orange extract
1 cup all-purpose flour
1 tsp. baking soda
½ tsp. salt

GANACHE
¼ cup half-and-half cream
3 oz. 53% cacao dark baking chocolate, coarsely chopped
   Optional: Fresh raspberries, confectioners' sugar and baking cocoa

1. Preheat oven to 350°. Pour boiling water over chocolate and butter; stir until smooth. Cool slightly. Whisk in sugar, buttermilk, egg and extracts. Combine flour, baking soda and salt; whisk into chocolate mixture just until blended.

2. Transfer to a 9-in. round baking pan coated with cooking spray. Bake until a toothpick inserted in center comes out clean, 18-22 minutes. Cool 10 minutes before removing from pan to a wire rack to cool completely. Place rack on a waxed paper-lined baking sheet.

3. For ganache, bring cream just to a boil in a small saucepan. Pour over chocolate; whisk until smooth. Cool until slightly thickened, about 10 minutes. Slowly pour over cake, allowing some ganache to drape over sides.

4. Refrigerate until serving. If desired, sprinkle with raspberries, confectioners' sugar and cocoa. Cut cake into wedges.

1 SLICE: 179 cal., 7g fat (4g sat. fat), 26mg chol., 236mg sod., 28g carb. (18g sugars, 1g fiber), 3g pro. **DIABETIC EXCHANGES:** 2 starch, 1 fat.

Chocolate Chip Dutch Baby

I modified a friend's traditional Dutch baby recipe to create this version.
My family thinks it's just terrific, and I love how easy it is.
—*Mary Thompson, LaCrosse, WI*

TAKES: 30 MIN. • MAKES: 4 SERVINGS

¼ cup miniature
semisweet
chocolate chips
¼ cup packed
brown sugar

DUTCH BABY
½ cup all-purpose flour
2 large eggs, room
temperature
½ cup half-and-half
cream
⅛ tsp. ground nutmeg
Dash ground cinnamon
3 Tbsp. butter
Optional: Maple syrup
and additional butter

SWEET SECRET
This recipe is plenty
sweet on its own, so
you may not even need
syrup. That said, you
can always spruce up
servings with fresh
raspberries or a dollop
of whipped cream.

1. In a small bowl, combine chocolate chips and brown sugar; set aside. In another small bowl, beat the flour, eggs, cream, nutmeg and cinnamon until smooth.

2. Place butter in a 9-in. pie plate or an 8-in. cast-iron skillet. Heat in a 425° oven until melted, about 4 minutes. Pour batter into hot pie plate or skillet. Sprinkle with chocolate chip mixture. Bake until top edges are golden brown, 13-15 minutes. Serve immediately, with syrup and butter if desired.

1 SLICE: 313 cal., 17g fat (10g sat. fat), 144mg chol., 140mg sod., 33g carb. (21g sugars, 1g fiber), 6g pro.

APPLE DUTCH BABY: Omit the chips, brown sugar, maple syrup and additional butter. Mix and bake Dutch baby as directed. Meanwhile, in a small saucepan, cook and stir 1 chopped peeled medium tart apple, ½ cup apple jelly and ⅛ tsp. ground cinnamon until jelly is melted. Top each slice with apple mixture.

FRUITED DUTCH BABY: Omit the chips, brown sugar, maple syrup and additional butter. Mix and bake Dutch baby as directed. Combine 2 sliced medium firm bananas and 1 cup sliced fresh strawberries. Top Dutch baby slices with fruit and, if desired, whipped cream;; sprinkle each serving with 1 Tbsp. toasted flaked coconut.

Chocolate-Dipped Beverage Spoons

These make cute gifts during the holidays. To set the chocolate quickly,
simply chill the dipped spoons in the freezer.
—*Marcy Boswell, Menifee, CA*

PREP: 45 MIN. + CHILLING • **MAKES:** 2 DOZEN

1   cup milk chocolate
    chips
3½ tsp. shortening, divided
1   cup white baking chips
24 metal or plastic spoons
    Optional: Coarse sugar
    or chocolate sprinkles

1. In a microwave-safe bowl, melt milk chocolate chips with 2 tsp. shortening; stir until smooth. Repeat with white baking chips and remaining shortening. Dip spoons into either mixture, tapping handles on bowl edges to remove excess. Place on a waxed paper-lined baking sheet. Chill for 5 minutes or until set.

2. Pipe or drizzle milk chocolate over white-dipped spoons and white mixture over milk chocolate-dipped spoons. Decorate with coarse sugar or sprinkles if desired. Chill for 5 minutes or until set. Use as stirring spoons for coffee or cocoa.

1 SPOON: 81 cal., 5g fat (3g sat. fat), 3mg chol., 12mg sod., 8g carb. (8g sugars, 0 fiber), 1g pro.

Quick & Easy Chocolate Sauce

Mom made this fudgy sauce to drizzle on cake, and we like it over ice cream, too.
It will keep for several weeks in the refrigerator.
—*Janice Miller, Creston, IA*

TAKES: 15 MIN. • **MAKES:** 2¼ CUPS

12 oz. (2 cups) semisweet
    chocolate chips
1   cup heavy
    whipping cream
¾ cup sugar

1. In a small heavy saucepan, combine all ingredients. Bring to a boil over medium heat, stirring constantly. Boil and stir 2 minutes.

2. Store in airtight containers in the refrigerator. Warm gently before serving.

2 TBSP.: 169 cal., 11g fat (6g sat. fat), 18mg chol., 7mg sod., 21g carb. (19g sugars, 1g fiber), 1g pro.

Chocolate Cherry Crepes

We suggest preparing the crepes and the filling in advance,
then you can assemble them and add the toppings just before serving.
—Taste of Home *Test Kitchen*

TAKES: 20 MIN. • MAKES: 6 SERVINGS

1   can (21 oz.) cherry pie
     filling
1   tsp. almond extract
⅔   cup 2% milk
2   large eggs
2   Tbsp. butter, melted
¼   cup blanched almonds,
     ground
¼   cup all-purpose flour

FILLING
1   cup heavy
     whipping cream
3   oz. semisweet
     chocolate, melted
     and cooled
¼   cup slivered almonds,
     toasted

1. In a small bowl, combine pie filling and almond extract; cover and refrigerate until chilled. For crepes, place the milk, eggs, butter, almonds and flour in a blender; cover and process until smooth.

2. Heat a lightly greased 8-in. nonstick skillet; pour about 2 Tbsp. batter into center of skillet. Lift and tilt pan to coat bottom evenly. Cook until top appears dry and bottom is golden brown; turn and cook 15-20 seconds longer. Remove to a wire rack. Repeat with remaining batter, greasing skillet as needed. Stack cooled crepes with waxed paper or paper towels in between.

3. For the filling, in a mixing bowl, beat cream and melted chocolate until soft peaks form. Spoon about 2 Tbsp. over each crepe; roll up. Top with cherry mixture and sprinkle with slivered almonds.

2 FILLED CREPES WITH TOPPINGS: 433 cal., 28g fat (14g sat. fat), 139mg chol., 108mg sod., 39g carb. (29g sugars, 2g fiber), 7g pro.

SWEET SECRET
Crepes are easy yet impressive. Once you get the hang of making them, you can use this crepe recipe and stuff them with any number of fillings. Go as simple as peaches and whipped cream or as complex as Boston cream pie custard.

Krisp Chocolate Sammie

This chocolaty sandwich is like a Saturday-morning breakfast without the bowl.
—*James Schend, Pleasant Prairie, WI*

TAKES: 5 MIN. • MAKES: 1 SERVING

1 Tbsp. creamy
    peanut butter
1 slice crusty
    white bread
2 Tbsp. Rice Krispies
1 tsp. grated dark
    chocolate candy bar

Spread peanut butter over bread. Top with Rice Krispies and chocolate.

1 OPEN-FACED SANDWICH: 195 cal., 10g fat (2g sat. fat), 0 chol., 229mg sod., 22g carb. (5g sugars, 2g fiber), 6g pro.

Glossy Chocolate Frosting

The original recipe for this thick chocolate frosting came from my grandmother.
I lightened it up, but it still has all the flavor and richness of Grandma's.
—*Melissa Wentz, Harrisburg, PA*

TAKES: 15 MIN. • MAKES: 1¼ CUPS

½ cup sugar
    Sugar substitute
    equivalent
    to ½ cup sugar
½ cup baking cocoa
3 Tbsp. cornstarch
1 cup cold water
4½ tsp. butter
1 tsp. vanilla extract

In a saucepan, combine the sugar, sugar substitute, cocoa and cornstarch. Add water and stir until smooth. Bring to a boil; cook and stir for 1 minute or until thickened. Remove from the heat; stir in the butter and vanilla until smooth. Spread over cupcakes, cakes or other baked goods while the frosting is still warm.

4 TSP.: 54 cal., 1g fat (1g sat. fat), 3mg chol., 12mg sod., 11g carb. (6g sugars, 1g fiber), 1g pro. **DIABETIC EXCHANGES:** ½ starch, ½ fat.

Black Forest Waffles

With their dark chocolate flavor and cherry and cream topping, these sensational waffles add a fancy touch to brunch with very little effort.
—*Edith Johnson, Fruita, CO*

TAKES: 30 MIN. • MAKES: 5 WAFFLES (ABOUT 6¾ IN.)

1 cup heavy whipping cream
3 Tbsp. confectioners' sugar
2 oz. unsweetened chocolate, chopped
3 Tbsp. shortening
1¾ cups cake flour
6 Tbsp. sugar
1 Tbsp. baking powder
½ tsp. salt
2 large eggs, separated
1 cup milk
1 can (21 oz.) cherry pie filling
  Chocolate sprinkles or fresh mint, optional

1. In a small bowl, beat cream until it begins to thicken. Add confectioners' sugar; beat until soft peaks form. Refrigerate until serving.

2. In a microwave, melt chocolate and shortening; stir until smooth. Cool slightly. In a large bowl, whisk flour, sugar, baking powder and salt. In another bowl, whisk egg yolks and milk until blended. Stir in chocolate mixture. Add to dry ingredients; stir just until moistened.

3. In a clean bowl, beat egg whites until stiff but not dry. Fold into batter. Bake in a preheated waffle iron according to manufacturer's directions until set.

4. Serve waffles with whipped cream and pie filling. If desired, top with sprinkles or fresh mint.

1 SERVING: 706 cal., 32g fat (16g sat. fat), 157mg chol., 567mg sod., 96g carb. (52g sugars, 2g fiber), 10g pro.

NOTES

_____
_____
_____
_____
_____
_____
_____
_____

Chocolate-Covered Cheesecake Squares

Satisfy your cheesecake craving with these bite-sized treats. Dipped in chocolate, the sweet, creamy delights are party favorites. But be warned...you won't be able to eat just one!
—*Esther Neustaeter, La Crete, AB*

PREP: 1½ HOURS + FREEZING • MAKES: 49 SQUARES

1 cup graham cracker crumbs
¼ cup finely chopped pecans
¼ cup butter, melted

FILLING
2 pkg. (8 oz. each) cream cheese, softened
½ cup sugar
¼ cup sour cream
2 large eggs, room temperature, lightly beaten
½ tsp. vanilla extract

COATING
24 oz. semisweet chocolate, chopped
3 Tbsp. shortening

1. Line a 9-in. square baking pan with foil and grease the foil. In a small bowl, combine the graham cracker crumbs, pecans and butter. Press into prepared pan; set aside.

2. In a large bowl, beat the cream cheese, sugar and sour cream until smooth. Add eggs and vanilla; beat on low speed just until combined. Pour over crust. Bake at 325° for 35-40 minutes or until center is almost set. Cool on a wire rack. Freeze overnight.

3. In a microwave, melt chocolate and shortening; stir until smooth. Cool slightly.

4. Using foil, lift cheesecake out of pan. Gently peel off foil; cut cheesecake into 1¼-in. squares. Work with a few pieces at a time for dipping; keep remaining squares refrigerated until ready to dip.

5. Using a toothpick, completely dip squares, 1 at a time, into melted chocolate; allow excess to drip off. Place on waxed paper-lined baking sheets. Spoon additional chocolate over the tops if necessary to coat. (Reheat chocolate if needed to finish dipping.) Let stand for 20 minutes or until set. Store in an airtight container in the refrigerator or freezer.

1 PIECE: 141 cal., 10g fat (6g sat. fat), 22mg chol., 48mg sod., 12g carb. (10g sugars, 1g fiber), 2g pro.

S'mores Stuffed French Toast

I had a craving for something sweet one morning, but all I had around the house was a handful of ingredients. This was the delicious outcome, and now I make it all the time.
—*Diana Palmer, Mammoth Cave, KY*

TAKES: 20 MIN. • **MAKES:** 4 SERVINGS

2 large eggs
1½ cups 2% milk
10 whole graham crackers, coarsely crushed (about 1¾ cups)
1 Tbsp. butter
8 slices French bread (¾ in. thick)
½ cup milk chocolate chips
½ cup miniature marshmallows
   Chocolate syrup, optional

1. In a wide shallow bowl, whisk eggs and milk until blended. Place graham cracker crumbs in another wide shallow bowl.

2. Grease a griddle with butter; heat over medium heat. Dip both sides of bread in egg mixture, then in crumbs, patting to help coating adhere. Place bread on griddle; toast until golden brown, 2-3 minutes on each side. Sprinkle chocolate chips and marshmallows over each of 4 toast slices; top with remaining toast. If desired, serve with chocolate syrup.

2 SLICES: 465 cal., 17g fat (8g sat. fat), 113mg chol., 526mg sod., 65g carb. (27g sugars, 3g fiber), 13g pro.,

SWEET SECRET
To minimize mess, use a rolling pin to crush graham crackers in the unopened sleeve, and try glass pie plates for dipping the bread into the eggs and crumbs.

Chocolate-Covered Bacon

A hit at state fairs everywhere, this salty-sweet concoction can be made at home.
Some say bacon can't get any better, but we think chocolate makes everything better!
—Taste of Home *Test Kitchen*

PREP: 20 MIN. • BAKE: 20 MIN. • MAKES: 1 DOZEN

12 thick-sliced bacon
   strips (about 1 lb.)
6 oz. white candy coating,
   coarsely chopped
   Optional toppings:
   Chopped dried apple
   chips, apricots and
   crystallized ginger;
   finely chopped pecans
   and pistachios; toasted
   coconut; kosher salt;
   brown sugar; cayenne
   pepper; and coarsely
   ground black pepper
1 cup semisweet
   chocolate chips
1 Tbsp. shortening

1. Preheat the oven to 400°. Carefully thread the bacon strips, weaving back and forth, onto twelve 12-in. soaked wooden skewers. Place on a rack in a large baking pan. Bake until crisp, 20-25 minutes. Drain on paper towels; cool bacon completely.

2. In a microwave, melt the white candy coating; stir until smooth. Brush onto both sides of 6 bacon strips; sprinkle with toppings as desired. Place on a waxed paper-lined baking sheet.

3. In a microwave, melt chocolate chips and shortening; stir until smooth. Brush onto both sides of remaining bacon; decorate as desired.

4. Refrigerate until set. Store in refrigerator.

1 PIECE: 212 cal., 14g fat (8g sat. fat), 10mg chol., 252mg sod., 19g carb. (17g sugars, 1g fiber), 5g pro.,

READER REVIEW
"Sweet and salty flavors go so well together and chocolate covered bacon is no exception! You can experiment with toppings. I used crystallized sugar to sprinkle on top of the bacon while the chocolate was setting, which turned out to be pretty and delicious."
—GLD2BMOM, TASTEOFHOME.COM

Chocolate Balloon Bowls

Enlist the kids to help make these DIY dessert bowls. They can be made ahead, so they're fabulous for birthday parties and holiday dinners.
—*Sarah Farmer, Waukesha, WI*

PREP: 20 MIN. + CHILLING • **MAKES:** 8 BOWLS

8 small balloons, filled with air and tied
24 oz. bittersweet chocolate, chopped, melted and cooled
6 oz. white baking chocolate, chopped, melted and cooled
Optional: Mousse, ice cream, sorbet, assorted fresh fruit and assorted candies

1. Clean balloons with a damp paper towel. Drop chocolate, 1 Tbsp. at a time, 2-3 in. apart on a parchment-lined baking sheet to make 8 circles. Pour the remaining bittersweet chocolate into a medium bowl.

2. Drizzle 1 Tbsp. white chocolate over bittersweet chocolate in bowl. Swirl with a toothpick or wooden skewer. Holding the tied end, carefully dip 1 balloon halfway into melted chocolate, rolling back and forth to coat; allow excess to drip off. Repeat with remaining balloons, adding 1 Tbsp. white chocolate and swirling before dipping each balloon.

3. To secure balloons, lightly press each, dipped side down, onto a chocolate circle; wait a few seconds before releasing pressure. Refrigerate until set, 5-10 minutes. Gently pop balloons; discard. Fill bowl as desired, with mousse, ice cream, sorbet, fresh fruit or candy.

1 BOWL: 592 cal., 36g fat (23g sat. fat), 0 chol., 15mg sod., 26g carb. (22g sugars, 4g fiber), 8g pro.

Chocolate Pecan Skillet Cookie

For variety, swap out the chocolate chips for an equal quantity of M&M's or chocolate chunks. Or, go fancy by mixing the chocolate chips and pecans into the dough, then gently folding in 1½ cups fresh raspberries.
—*James Schend, Pleasant Prairie, WI*

PREP: 15 MIN. • **BAKE:** 35 MIN. • **MAKES:** 12 SERVINGS

1 **cup butter**
1 **cup sugar**
1 **cup packed brown sugar**
2 **large eggs, room temperature**
2 **tsp. vanilla extract**
3 **cups all-purpose flour**
1½ **tsp. baking soda**
½ **tsp. kosher salt**
1 **cup 60% cacao bittersweet chocolate baking chips**
1 **cup chopped pecans, toasted**
Vanilla ice cream, optional

1. Preheat oven to 350°. In a 12-in. cast-iron skillet, heat butter in oven as it preheats. Meanwhile, in a large bowl, stir together sugar and brown sugar. When the butter is almost melted, remove skillet from oven and swirl butter until completely melted. Stir butter into sugar mixture; set skillet aside.

2. Beat eggs and vanilla into sugar mixture. In another bowl, whisk together flour, baking soda and salt; gradually beat into sugar mixture. Stir in chocolate chips and nuts. Spread mixture into buttered skillet.

3. Bake until toothpick inserted in center comes out with moist crumbs and top is golden brown, 35-40 minutes. Serve warm, with vanilla ice cream if desired.

1 SERVING: 528 cal., 27g fat (13g sat. fat), 72mg chol., 378mg sod., 69g carb. (43g sugars, 3g fiber), 6g pro.

NOTES

Recipe Index